God You've Never Met

Who is the Holy Spirit?

NIKKI ROMANI

FOREWORD BY HAVILAH CUNNINGTON

Cover design by Nikki Romani
Artwork by Danielle Dumas
Digital art by Mark Sidenfaden
Editor Anna Floit
Formatting by Scott Cuzzo

Nikkiromani.com

ISBN: 9781659851960

Dedicated to my Grandma.

Someone who knew the
Holy Spirit and lived her
life with Him daily.
I miss you!

Contents

Foreword

If you have been in the church very long, you have likely heard common phrases used concerning the Holy Spirit. They usually sound something like, "He lives in me" or "The Holy Spirit moved." We also call Him by many names. But in this book, Nikki's experiences challenge us to ask ourselves if we really know Him. Most of us know He is called the Comforter, but have we let Him comfort us? Jesus called Him the Helper, yet we can still have great difficulty letting go of our own control long enough to see His guidance come through. A few of us may have grown content believing He's unassuming, quiet, or mysterious. Even more of us have stopped asking questions altogether. But what if there's more?

I first met Nikki at a friend's house. As I listened to her story, it was evident she was a woman of adventure, who was passionate about coloring outside the lines. A few months later, she came to my mind again. It was that nudge, which led me to give Nikki a word I heard God speaking over her life. I heard Him saying, "You're going to introduce people to a God they've never met. It might sound crazy, but for many, the Holy Spirit may need an introduction."

Since then, I've watched a fire blaze a trail of destiny in her life. Nikki has a revelatory gift that enables the world around her to more clearly comprehend Who the Holy Spirit is and why we need Him in our lives.

Without the Holy Spirit, I would not be where I am today. When I was 17, I was on my way to a party when I felt Holy Spirit convict my heart by saying, "There is more to life than this! I have called you. Come follow me." Since that moment, I have valued the voice of the Holy Spirit in my life, and the ways He speaks to me. He's led me into encounters; taught me how to communicate to multitudes; showed me the way to lead a ministry; counseled me on how to love my husband and family well, and how to live a victorious life daily.

But I don't have an exclusive relationship with Him reserved for only those in ministry. This kind of life, led by the Holy Spirit, is for everyone.

So how do we connect with this part of God? Nikki answers those questions we often have bouncing around in our heads. If you are on a journey to understanding Who the Holy Spirit is, and what it looks like to have Him in your life, this book is for you. Nikki's words are a megaphone for the truth about the Holy Spirit. As a logical and strong thinker herself, Nikki shamelessly walks the reader through her personal encounters with the Holy Spirit that might surprise even the most cynical of readers. Her vulnerability shakes off the modern-day veil that hides the Third Person of the Trinity, who can often be regarded as distant, elusive, or even written off as "strange."

Her simple words carry their weight as she expounds the Scripture and shares miraculous stories from her life that will undoubtedly create a hunger to see them happen in your own life.

Nikki's voice is a call to action, not just information. This book will leave you asking yourself, "Do I really know Him as

He wants to be known?" It will make merely knowing about Him unsatisfying, and frankly, uncomfortable. When you truly know someone, your life reflects that relationship. Her stories reveal the fruit of knowing the Holy Spirit and invites us to experience the same.

Nikki will walk you through the process of connecting with the Holy Spirit in a raw, beautiful way as she introduces you to The God You've Never Met. He will change your life forever, just as He's changed ours.

Havilah Cunnington, author of *Stronger Than the Struggle* and founder of **Truth to Table**

A God You've Never Met: Who is the Holy Spirit?

Introduction

Stories are captivating. They help you relate and feel as though you can experience whatever the story is about for yourself. Stories help bring insight and understanding. My grandma was good at that. It seemed as though she had a story for every situation. Grandma was a senior pastor in her day, and as I look through her notes for sermons, or letters to friends, she always shared a story to make a point or explain a lesson.

Connections are created through stories. They are relatable. Jesus taught with stories and I want to share stories with you about experiences with the Holy Spirit. I want to connect with you, relate to you, bring you in and share with you a God you've never met. At one point in my life I didn't know Him either, and I continue to learn more about Him with each new day.

Along with these stories, I will highlight some of the many scriptures about the Holy Spirit. My prayer is that you take what you read and seek it out for yourself. Don't solely take my word for it, test it. Don't live off of others' experiences. Experience it for yourself. Take ownership of your beliefs. That's exactly what I needed to do myself. The stories I had heard from others about the Holy Spirit I wanted for myself. I realized for many years I was hanging onto others' beliefs and who they said God was and didn't have much of my own understanding. It requires risk. It requires stepping out of your comfort zone. It requires taking God out of a box. It requires opening up your mind to the impossible. It requires stepping into the unknown. But let me tell you, when you do, you will not be disappointed.

> *"A man with an argument has no power over a man with experience."*

Kris Vallotton

My prayer and hope as you read this book is that it ignites a desire within you to know more and seek more of the Holy Spirit. I pray as you read through these pages you open up to a world you may not have known before or gain more of an understanding. I am not an expert by any means, but God has given me this opportunity to share my life with you and who the Holy Spirit is to me.

About 6 years ago, I received a message from a family friend, Havilah Cunnington, whom I had seen at my best friend's wedding. At the wedding she and I were able to talk briefly, and she asked what was going on in my life. At the time I was trying to figure it out. I was in the process of deciding whether or not to go to graduate school, or if God had something else in mind.

This was the message she sent me in January 2013:

> *"For what it's worth I felt led by the Lord to encourage you with this. He sees you. He loves you and He's proud of you. He is working on*

you and your calling. I believe He's going to be speaking to you in a clearer way in this next season. I see Him giving you more direction on what you are to be doing and the specific calling you have. I see you traveling more and leading with love to others. You are going to be a secret weapon for Him. You will look harmless to those you are coming to help but spiritually you will be taking them to places they've never been, meeting a God they've never met. God says to ask Him for more courage in your daily life to live out your destiny."

I have referred back to this word time and time again. When I was thinking of what the title of this book should be, God brought me back to this message, and I knew this was it.

I want to introduce you to a God you've never met.

A God You've Never Met: Who is the Holy Spirit?

Chapter 1

The Fear of Losing Control

There I was, rolling around on the floor, unable to control myself, and not wanting to if I could. As tears of joy streamed down my face, I looked up at my friend Rachel, who was standing over me, as she asked, "Can you believe this is happening to you?"

I responded as I caught my breath, "No I can't!"

This was the moment I had a true encounter with a God I'd never met.

You see, I grew up in the church. I faithfully attended youth group and Christian schools, but never fully surrendered my life to Jesus for fear of losing control. Looking back, I now realize my life has been a series of divine appointments with a God I'd never met pursuing me and showing me what life would be like with Him in the driver's seat. I knew about God, Jesus, and the Holy Spirit forming the Trinity, but I never allowed myself to truly understand their unique roles;

I was in a church community who didn't talk about the Holy Spirit's character. Something seemed to be missing as I learned more about God and Jesus. Things didn't line up with the stories in the Bible about the Holy Spirit's presence and even my Grandma's stories. As a child I didn't understand the importance of her stories. I didn't know there was a God I'd never met, even though I'd always heard about Him outside of this church community. At some point, these stories became not only stories from the Bible and Grandma, but real-time stories from people about their own miracles, unexplainable healings, and angel sightings. All these people had one thing in common. They'd let go of control of their own lives. For so long, I wasn't ready to do that.

I had what I thought was a relationship with Jesus throughout high school and college, knowing and believing He was real, but never really learning about the power of the Holy Spirit—most likely because I didn't want to. The Holy Spirit was someone I would read about in the Bible, one part of the Trinity, but I never truly understood His role and didn't take it upon myself to learn. I believed the Holy Spirit was someone who would take control of people and made strange, uncomfortable stuff happen.

I will never forget my camp experience in seventh grade, when my cousin Erynne and I traveled to Oregon to stay at Camp Crestview. During worship one night, as we stood in a room full of campers and counselors and as the worship team led us through our songs from the stage, the camp staff walked around the room laying hands on certain people, who then fell on their backs to the floor. I heard languages I had never heard before being spoken around me, and I was afraid. I hoped nobody would see me, because I didn't want to be touched and fall on the ground too. I had no idea what was going on. No one had ever explained it to me.

That night scared me, and the experience wasn't mentioned again until about twelve years later at a Bible study, when the Holy Spirit took control of my body in the way I was once afraid of. I didn't realize it until I was older, but I had put a wall up to this part of the Trinity, whom I later learned was the Holy Spirit. I was fearful and wanted to remain in control of my body. I believe this is one of the reasons I remained stagnant in my faith for a period of my life. I wasn't growing in my relationship with God. I had put a barrier between me and the power of the Holy Spirit.

I grew up with a dad who is a perfectionist and likes to be in control. He likes things his way. He has his home in order, just the way he wants it and works hard to keep it that way. I think to some extent we all like to be in control. We want our lives to operate a certain way, and giving up that control to someone else is scary. I think a lot of people have trouble with this when it relates to God. Because of my camp experience in the seventh grade and living with a dad who modeled what it looks like to be in control and maintain order, I struggled with giving God my whole life. I would only give Him pieces. I would tell Him, *You can have this portion, but not that.* Even though I saw the pain and stress my dad experienced trying to keep control, I had a hard time giving up control myself. I have a lot in common with my dad.

The night I found myself rolling on the ground changed everything for me. That was the moment I wanted all in, and I let go of control to the point my body was literally on the ground while I laughed uncontrollably. You would not expect this from someone who wanted to keep control. But something changed in me that night, and throughout this book I will share my journey with you of how I got to this point in hopes you will too. I wish for you to experience this God you've never met. Trust me when I say once you experience this God, you will be forever changed and never want to turn back.

Chapter 2

The Fear of Rejection

I see the best in people. I see an individual's true potential. I see who they could be. I would say this is a gift, but sometimes it has gotten me into unfortunate situations. I am also a peacemaker and desire for everyone to get along. I initiate conversation if something needs to be sorted out, and like to get to the bottom of a problem so people can live in harmony. Because I seek this harmony, I too want to be accepted by others.

When I was in elementary school, I understood one particular girl was the ringleader of my group of friends. She had two sides to her. She seemed nice and could put on a smile, but on the flip side she was persuasive, manipulative, and often convinced us to break the rules. Something about her drew people in and they wanted to be liked by her. I was with Lexi the one and only time I was sent to the principal's office. I never broke the rules, but on this occasion, she and some other girls had the bright idea of carving into a tree at recess. I was skeptical about the whole thing, but I wanted to be a part of the group, so if they were doing it, I would too. Honestly, I don't even remember actually carving into the tree, but I stood there as a witness. We got caught and were sent to the principal. Once in the office, we stood with our noses to the wall around the room to prevent us from talking to each other. One by one, we were brought in front of the principal to plead our case. I was mortified. This was the worst trouble I had ever gotten into and I didn't want it to ever happen again.

After this incident, I kept my distance from Lexi. I found friends who didn't want to follow her, because all she did was cause trouble. This divided our little elementary group. It was heartbreaking because I lost some friends over it. I tried to tell Lexi what she was doing was wrong, but that made her not like me. I saw the person she could be—a leader—but she was leading people in the wrong direction and I didn't want to be a part of it. I tell you this because I went against my morals to be liked and accepted. I feared being judged. I wanted others to like me. I didn't want to seem weird or different from the others. I also saw the best in those around me and wanted all of us to get along and be a happy friend group again. That didn't happen.

As an elementary school girl, teenager, and even young adult, I continued this need for acceptance. I wouldn't raise my hands in worship for fear of what others might say. I wouldn't pray out loud for fear of being judged for saying the wrong thing. I'm not saying I have it all together now—I still struggle with this at times. However, I am less concerned with what others think of me and more about what God thinks of me.

This happened over time, and with the growth of my desire to know this God I'd never met, because He started to show up in unexpected ways.

He showed up unexpectedly when I was in eighth grade. In that moment, I didn't care what others thought. In that moment, I stood in chapel, singing praise songs to God with my hands raised, feeling as though it was just me and Jesus in the room. What made this moment different? Did it remind me of those days at summer camp when I was surrounded by kids who wanted to be there? Who wanted to worship God? Did it remind me of those surrendered corporate worship times while I was on mission trips to Mexico with my youth group?

In the midst of my fear of being accepted, something changed in that moment and I didn't care what others thought of me. That encounter with God was another piece to the puzzle of learning more about the Holy Spirit.

I was in an unhealthy relationship with a boy. This relationship started when we were juniors in high school—young love. This boy first asked me to be his girlfriend when we were sophomores, but I told him I was too young. This makes me laugh now, but I realize the Holy Spirit had a hold of my heart even from the start, and He was protecting me. It wasn't until junior year we began to date. He was someone I had known since eighth grade. We were best friends, but something changed, and I became attracted to him in more than a friend kind of way.

Over the years, our families became really close, to the point we went on family vacations together, so it just made sense he and I should be together. When we were seventeen, we talked about getting married and how perfect it would be because our families were already like family. However, something tugged at me in those moments of discussion and I got a feeling this was not what should happen. I brushed those feelings aside, but the reason I didn't want to go through with it was because I was set on going to college in San Diego. At that point, he was in the army and stationed on the other side of the country. If we got married, I would have to move, but because I was so set on going to college, not even this boy was going to change that.

He was a "bad" boy according to my morals and upbringing, but this is what intrigued me. I was a rule follower. Something about him being a rule breaker excited me. I wasn't willing to rebel, but I reasoned that if I was with someone who was, it would seem as though I were a part of that world. Being the good Christian girl that I was, it was out of my character to be with a guy like him. All the girls wanted to date him, but he chose me! Or so I thought.

Throughout our relationship, I looked past all the wrong and saw the best in him. I thought I could be a positive influence and help him change to become who God created him to be. This was not my responsibility, though I had put it upon myself. My friends told me he was not a good guy. Honestly, not many people understood why I was with him. But I saw who he *could* be. I saw his potential. He was young and trying to figure life out, but I made excuses for him and how he treated me. He cheated on me and wasn't supportive of me and my dreams. He was manipulative and disrespectful. Yet, I chose not to see those things.

Throughout all of this, something deep down was tugging on my heart to get out of this relationship. After almost a year of ignoring all the signs, I found us sitting on opposite sides of the jacuzzi one night, and something within me started to break up with him. It was as though someone was putting the words into my mouth. He finally asked, "Are you breaking up with me?" To which I responded, "I think I am."

The next day, I was such a wreck, I couldn't get out of bed. *What did I just do?* I had the pain of losing someone I loved, but deep down I knew it was right. It wasn't until a few months later I realized the Holy Spirit inside of me was the One who had broken up with him. He was the One tugging on my heart. He was the One who put the strong desire in me to go to college. He was protecting me. This realization awoke something within me. I became aware of how God was pursuing me and was always with me. Was there more to this God I had learned about as a child?

Perhaps you've experienced similar kinds of moments in your life. I was holding onto the fear of being rejected in that relationship. I was holding onto the goodness I saw in my boyfriend. But that fear of rejection and holding onto this dream of his true potential ended up causing me pain, heartache, and hindered me from growing in my relationship with God. Now I see God was with me. Through my healing I have seen the ways the Holy Spirit was guiding me. I do not regret that relationship. I have learned many valuable lessons from the experience. I still care and want the best for this guy because you never forget your first love. However, I had to let him go and allow God to do what He needed to do in his life.

Take a moment to look back on your life and see where the Holy Spirit was at work. During the pain and the heartache, you may not have realized what He was up to. Ask Him to show you where He was in those moments. I did this years later as I reflected on this relationship and worked through healing the pain and rejection I had experienced as a teenager. Now I see the Holy Spirit all over it! He was with me the whole time, but I chose not to see Him until the Holy Spirit made Himself so clear He was impossible to miss! He was the One who told me to wait to date until I was a junior. He was the One who put the desire in my heart to say no to marriage and go to college. He was the One who put friends in my life to help me see what was really going on. He was the One who broke up with my boyfriend for me.

The Holy Spirit is the One who fully accepts me for who I am and loves me just the same. I don't need the approval of others around me. I don't need to betray my beliefs and morals to be a part of this world. It's not my responsibility to fix people. I am no one's savior. I am a child of God, living my life for Him, and that is all that matters.

Chapter 3

The Fear of Not Being the "Perfect" Christian

What does it mean to be a Christian? There are many denominations, many ways to worship. But the most important aspect is to be Christ followers. We need to take the religion out of it and live in *relationship*. If you know this God I'm talking about, you know He wants you and He loves you. He tells us to love Him and love our neighbor as ourselves. That's it. Why have we become so wrapped up in the logic and religion? I'll admit I did too.

I grew up in a split home. My parents are still married, but my mom is a believer and my dad is not. Throughout my childhood, my siblings and I went to church with Mom while Dad stayed home. Every Sunday I asked Dad if he wanted to go with us, and each time he had an excuse for why he couldn't or wouldn't go. This confused me as a child. It was hard for me to understand why my dad didn't want to go with us. I would see friends of mine with both parents at church and longed for the same. As I got older, I realized how hard this was for my mom, even harder than it was for me.

My parents' differing beliefs created a divide in the home. Dad has never understood why we do things we feel God has called us to, and it's hard for me to understand why he won't believe in this God the rest of us love and follow. Despite his unbelief, Dad wanted us kids to attend private Christian schools, which I am grateful for. He was fine with us going to church and believing in God, he just didn't want to participate himself.

I have my mom to thank for why I am a follower of Jesus. If it weren't for her taking us to church and showing us who God is, who knows what my life would be today. However, going to church was non- negotiable. We kids had to go to church with Mom, and I am forever grateful we did.

My mom says she chose the conservative church we attended because the youth group was so amazing. I agree with her; it was! However, very few people raised their hands during the praise and worship. It was far from what you might know as charismatic. There was order and structure, a beautiful choir and orchestra, and sometimes the organ would be played. From the pulpit, there was mention of the trinity; God the Father, Jesus the Son, and the Holy Spirit; but not much mention of the Holy Spirit's role and exactly who He was. He was just a part of the trinity, and God's spirit would "fall upon" people, but I didn't know what that meant.

I did love the church I grew up in. I looked forward to going every Sunday because my friends were there, the people were nice, I felt accepted and loved—and yet something was missing—a kind of power we only read about in the Bible.

Growing up as a Christian, I had the impression there were rules to follow, commandments to live by. And being the rule follower that I am, I tried my best to stick to these rules. I wanted to be viewed as the "perfect" Christian. But with that came stress and not taking risks for fear of messing up or not being perceived as what I thought a Christian looked like. That's way too much pressure for one person.

I realized I needed to figure out what I believed, not what others had taught me over the years. I knew I wanted to be a good person, have strong morals, and it was in my nature to follow the rules. However, I was still focused on the religion rather than the relational aspect. Something huge was missing. I had put the pressure of being perceived as the "perfect" Christian upon myself which soon became too much to bear.

Looking back, I realize I was a *fan* of Jesus, not a *disciple*. I went to church, attended Christian events and church trips, and studied Bible class at my Christian private school; it was as though I was in a celebrity fan club. I think of the day I joined Mary-Kate and Ashley Olsen's fan club when I was eleven years old. I came home from school and walked into the house to find a box on the kitchen table. I knew immediately what it was. I ran to it and began jumping up and down, screaming with excitement.

I loved who I thought Mary-Kate and Ashley were. I had all their movies, watched their shows, and now I was a member of their fan club. What more could an eleven-year-old girl want? I opened the box to find autographed pictures of the sisters, posters, and other goodies. I didn't know them personally, but I felt as though I did, because I was a fan. This is how my relationship with Jesus was. I liked the idea of him, but I didn't truly *know* him.

When I turned twenty-one, I had my first alcoholic beverage. Yes, I was one of those kids who waited until twenty-one to drink. I was a rule follower, remember? At twenty-one, I could go to clubs and buy alcohol. I had a few drunk nights, enough to know what it was like, and enough to know I hated how I felt the next day. My parents unknowingly put pressure on me to sustain a good reputation with the people around me. I rarely saw my parents drink alcohol, so when I did, they said things such as, "You will lose your good reputation." "What will others think of you now?"

I'm not a parent myself, but I can only imagine what it would be like to see your child drink alcohol for the first time. It might come as a shock, because you realize your baby is an adult and can make decisions for him- or herself. I don't blame my parents for what they said. I did have a desire to be perceived as "perfect," and hold onto that "good reputation." Deep down I cared what they thought about me, and what others thought as well and wanted to keep to the rules of the "religion" I was following.

Each time I did something against what I knew to be the "right" decision, I felt convicted. Nevertheless, it's not about whether I consider things to be good or bad. It's not even about behavior. It's not about following certain rules; it's about following the Holy Spirit.

Jesus had a hold of my life since I was six years old. When you invite Jesus into your life, and the Holy Spirit enters your heart, He never leaves. He never distances Himself. You may feel at times that He is far away, but it's up to you to turn around and see Him. This is what it was like for me. Looking back, I see Jesus was always with me, waiting for me to dive into a relationship with Him. I never took the time to get to know Him. In those moments when I felt like something was wrong, it was the Holy Spirit telling me I was going in the opposite direction of where He was leading me.

We as humans have over complicated what it means to be a Christian. It's simple; we need to take the religion out of it and focus on the relationship. Our main goal in life is to love the Lord our God with all our hearts and love our neighbors as ourselves, and the rest will fall into place. Yet there's an aspect to this we have access to and are not utilizing. His name is the Holy Spirit.

What does it mean to be a Christ follower? It means to have the Holy Spirit living within you. He is our guide, our counselor. Jesus tells His disciples,

> I will ask the Father, and he will give you another Counselor to be with you forever—the Spirit of truth. The world cannot accept him, because it neither sees him nor knows him. But you know him, for he lives with you and will be in you.

John 14:16-17

Once I began to learn more about the Holy Spirit and realize His role, and focus on the relationship aspect, the more whole I've felt, the more I do not strive for the approval of others as long as I have His. The more I could let go of whatever reputation I was holding onto.

I have been able to live my life as Jesus wants me to. Others may not always agree, but if you are in line with God's provision for your life, nothing else matters. This is what I came to realize. It's not about what my parents think of me.

It's not about what others think of me. It's about what God thinks of me. I want to live my life for Him and no one else.

The Holy Spirit is the One I have lived most of my life not knowing much about and not realizing He has been with me the entire time. He is the One we are to follow. He will tell you what to do. Let's start focusing on our relationship with God and less on religion. Let's follow the Holy Spirit and start realizing how much God wants a relationship with us. Let go of the idea of what a "perfect" Christian looks like and look to Jesus' example for us as He lived His life on earth, seeking His Heavenly Father, and being led by the Holy Spirit.

Chapter 4

The Thief Called Comparison

I surround myself with people who are one or a few steps in front of me in my faith. Two things can happen in this situation. One, they can push you to pursue God and create a deeper relationship with Him. Or two, you begin to compare yourself to them, thinking they have a better relationship and are more in tune with the Holy Spirit than you. In the past, I started to do the latter. I found a certain friend was more prophetic, would get the "Holy Spirit shakes," and spoke in tongues. I wanted what she had, but I began to compare myself to her and eventually let comparison take over and I shut down. I began to view her as a little "out there," a little too "into the spirit." I never said these thoughts aloud to her, because a part of me was envious.

Comparison is the thief of joy. This is exactly what happened to me. I am usually a joyful person, but when I saw her shake or speak in tongues I would raise my eyebrows and think, *Pff, what are you doing?*

I was too much in my head. I was trying to think logically and realistically. I was frustrated with myself. Part of this behavior was due to unbelief. I had not grown up around spiritual gifts such as prophecy, tongues, and healing, so I didn't know what to think of it all. I am a thinker. I even scored as such on the Myers-Briggs test. I like facts and details. The ways of the Holy Spirit did not make sense to me, and because of this I allowed a wall to form between He and I, and as a result, I projected this lack onto my friend.

Emotions are hard for me to express. This may be another reason why I made excuses to not dive deeper into a relationship with the Holy Spirit and not allow Him to work in and through my life, because deep down I knew I would have to deal with the emotions I had stuffed away and not dealt with. I compared myself to others in this sense too. Those who seemed to have a handle on the emotion thing, who were able to express their emotions with words, I would keep at a distance. It was as though when I was around these people, the joy was sucked out of me. I couldn't handle them and everything in me wanted to walk away.

Over time, I realized I was comparing myself to my friend and her giftings from the Spirit that I didn't have. I realized I was not only running from my own emotions, but from the emotions of others as well. I eventually reached out to this friend of mine and asked for help. I wanted what she had, but instead of comparing, I was honest with her and told her what I thought was really going on. Because of my honesty and vulnerability, my view of the Holy Spirit changed. I began to ask more questions. I became more open to His role. I started to release my façade of having it all together. I wanted more, and because of this I was able to experience Him in a radical way.

Surround yourself with people one or a few steps ahead of you in their relationship with God. Allow them to push you closer to Jesus. Don't let comparison get in the way! There is only one you. You are unique, as am I. I am the only me in this whole world. I am the only one with the giftings I have. I am the only one who can take responsibility for my relationship with the Holy Spirit. If I want to be used by Him, I must take ownership.

A God You've Never Met: Who is the Holy Spirit?

Chapter 5

The Fear of Vulnerability

I have been on a journey while writing this book. To start, it was one of the toughest seasons of my life to date. At the beginning of the year, I asked God what the upcoming year would look like. Some people choose a word or words to describe the year they are stepping into. I really felt as though God was telling me this was going to be a year of preparation and healing. And that is exactly what happened! As soon as God shared this with me, I fell into a state of depression. Not what you were expecting, right?

I didn't know what it was at first. I was tired all the time, low on energy, didn't want to get myself out of bed, and didn't want to be around people. However, when I was around others, I hid this part of me well, so no one knew what was going on. I am a girl who doesn't really talk about emotions anyway. I am all about the facts and getting straight to the point. I am still this way, and that's ok, but I realize it is also ok to let people into the mess.

I realize now the Holy Spirit was with me because although I was isolating myself as much as I could, I never felt alone. At the time, I was being discipled by a woman and she was the one who identified the depression. I was trying to run from the "D" word because I didn't want to be identified as a "depressed person." I never wanted to identify with any negative emotion, for that matter, because I thought I would stay in that state forever. I know, a little unrealistic. However, once she told me I was depressed, I was determined to get past it. I heard someone once say, "If you are in hell, you shouldn't want to stay there. You need to get out so keep going!" And that's exactly what I needed to do.

During this season, I gained self-awareness and began to realize I was using exercise and food as an escape, which I had done my whole life! This caused me to suppress my feelings and not deal with them if they were anything other than joy and positivity. I would escape the task of dealing with my unknown emotions by going to the gym or for a run or eating something comforting. Once I became aware of the problem, I identified the cycle I fell into. Emotion approaches, go to the gym.

Emotion still there, go for a run or eat. It worked for a while, but over time it caught up with me.

Within these first few months of the year, God told me to stop using exercise as a way to numb the pain. In fact, He told me to stop working out all together for four weeks. Unless it was a walk to sort through my thoughts, no working out. This sounded crazy to me, but it was something I needed to do to start the process of sorting through my emotions and dealing with them. So, I did it. Out of obedience, I decided to sit in my emotions and journal and have quiet time with Jesus. It wasn't easy. Sometimes I would just sit there and have no clue what to do. But I did what I do best and wrote whatever came to my mind, which truly helps so much, to actually write with a pen in your own handwriting.

When the four weeks were up, I started to feel much better. I made an agreement with God and myself that I had to deal with the emotion at hand and then I could exercise. Exercise became a reward and soon something I looked forward to instead of an escape route. By March of that same year, I was stepping out of depression, thanks to my confidant the Holy Spirit, my discipler, and my determination. However, I knew I had deep-rooted issues I still needed to bring to the surface. I made the decision to go to counseling that August. At first, I didn't know what to expect. I had never been to counseling before. I just knew in order to become a better me, I needed professional help. I knew I had unresolved feelings, but I didn't know what they were or how to present them. I was unable to identify any emotions (other than joy) or what I was feeling. I couldn't find the words. All I knew was I avoided them at all costs. Over two decades of stuffing emotions caught up with me. Now it was time to deal. Insert therapy.

I have heard pastors compare our lives to a house with many rooms. At first the comparison didn't make sense. It wasn't until I took time to really think about this analogy that God gave me a new perspective. My life and your life are houses. My house looks different than yours, but all the same it has many rooms. Some of my rooms have been closed and dark with no lights on or windows open. And it wasn't until going to therapy that I started opening the doors to those rooms. As I walked inside, I was disgusted with what I saw. They were dark and dirty, but I walked over to the windows to open them and pulled back the curtains to start cleaning. Such a messy process.

Sometimes equipment is needed, such as a vacuum, a broom, a dustpan, and cleaning spray. I view this equipment as therapy tools: journaling, reflecting, and talking with trusted family and friends about the situation—whatever you need to do to clean out those rooms and let the light in! Vulnerability is hard, but vulnerability is all a part of the cleaning process. And we cannot let the fear of letting people into our mess and letting Jesus into our mess stop us. When we open the doors to those rooms, the Holy Spirit will flood in and fill them. And that's when we become whole.

I am learning how to be vulnerable, which is why I believe God is telling me to share this part of my story with you. Vulnerability is actually courage and not weakness, according to Brene´ Brown, who says, "It's the willingness to show up and be seen with no guarantee of outcome."[1] Brene´ defines shame as "the intensely painful feeling or experience of believing we are flawed and therefore unworthy of acceptance and belonging."[2] I am finding this to be true.

When I tell people what is going on internally, I become more relatable and trustworthy. I don't have to act like everything is ok when it's not. This is something I have been doing ever since I can remember. I would pretend to be ok all the time. I would be joyful and happy because that's what I thought living a life with Jesus was supposed to look like. Wrong! It's hard. It has its ups and downs. We are in a battle. But one thing remains true, God is constant, and He will never leave. He is our hope.

This is not to say I am not a joyful person. I am! It's because of the hope I have in Jesus. I smile all the time and enjoy making people laugh, but this doesn't mean I never experience sadness, anger, or frustration. I am human. And

1   *Rising Strong* Brene Brown

2   Brene Brown *I thought it was just me but it isn't: Making the Journey from "What people think?" to "I am enough."*

one of the many things I've learned while in therapy is God has emotions too—something I guess I was blind to seeing before. I read the Bible with new eyes now and see all kinds of emotions revealed. It's kind of a relief! My new motto is *It's ok not to be ok all the time*, which is something I have to remind myself daily.

One month after the resolution of my depression, and before I started my therapy journey, God told me to write this book. I didn't know writing something like this would help me with my healing process, but it has. God knew. The Holy Spirit reminded me He has been with me the entire time. I know this because I reflected on the events that occurred and realized His strategic placement of certain people in my life and specific tasks He wanted me to complete, such as reading through the Old Testament and writing this book.

The Holy Spirit is the One who has walked with me through the pain and the struggle. He is the One who is healing me. He is the One who made me feel as though I was not alone. He brought people into my life to support me, love me, pray for me, and encourage me along the way. And He continues to do all this and more. I was making excuses for putting this portion of my story in the book because, hello vulnerability! But I want freedom and with freedom comes the ability to share the hard parts of your story along with the good and see where the Holy Spirit fits into it all.

God gave me a vision during my time of pain and struggle and I believe He gave it to me to pull me out of the pit I was in. I was standing on stage speaking to hundreds of people. My appearance was of someone who was confident, fit, healthy, and strong. I was radiating and had the biggest smile on my face as I shared something of encouragement to the people in front of me.

This is the picture I come back to while on this journey. I feel as though the Holy Spirit was sharing with me who I am made to be, and I have been on a mission ever since to become that girl. Life is a process and continuation of growth. We should never be stagnant. God wants us to have a life of abundance and to be the person He created us to be. Are you on the path to becoming that person?

Chapter 6

Releasing Control

In the summer of 2012, my friend Rachel and I took a month-long trip. We traveled to Costa Rica for the first part of the month and met up with our church group in Nicaragua at the end. Our time in Costa Rica was fun and full of adventure, with much needed rest. In those moments, Rachel would ask me questions such as, "Who is God to you?" And for some reason, it was a hard question for me to answer. I decided I needed to utilize my time of rest and dive into the Word of God.

Reading my Bible was not something I did on a regular basis, nonetheless it was something I wanted to incorporate into my daily routine. In a way, I was overwhelmed and did not know where to begin. As I shared earlier, I grew up going to church, so I had "heard all the stories," but this time I wanted to read it for myself with fresh eyes, and listen for God to speak to me. Praying for God to show up in a new way and speak to me from His Word was exactly what I needed to pray during that month, and He answered. I was ready to become a disciple of Jesus, no longer a fan.

This may be helpful for you if you do not know where to start. Here's what I did. I started reading 1 John, about God's love for His children. I jumped to the book of John and read about the birth and life of Jesus here on earth. When I read, it was as though I was reading it for the first time, and I gained a better understanding. These were stories I had heard a million times, but something was different this time around. Maybe it was the increase in my desire for more. Maybe out of desperation I really took to heart the words I was reading. Whatever it was, God spoke to me through His living Word.

I read my Bible every day while in Central America. I journaled all I was learning, and answered Rachel's questions, even if it was uncomfortable and hard at times. Something shifted in me on that trip. This was the start of my new beginning to become a disciple of Jesus. I became more open to the role of the Holy Spirit and the gifts He gives us. I was gaining a new understanding of what it means to be a Christ follower. And God gave me my first vision on this trip.

At the end of the summer, Rachel invited me to a Bible study with people from her university.[3] Honestly, I did not want to go. She had told me stories of people at this Bible study experiencing the Holy Spirit in radical ways, giving me flashbacks to seventh grade summer camp, and I didn't want anything to do with it. Needless to say, I was afraid. So when I said I was becoming more "open" to the role of the Holy Spirit, it was under my terms. I was not ready to release control just yet.

Rachel was not taking no for an answer. To compromise, I told her I would drive myself and meet her there, to give myself an out so I could leave whenever I wanted. When I arrived, the leader, Bob, greeted me with Rachel standing next

3   August 2012, Azusa Pacific University

to him. He shook my hand and said, "I heard you are nervous about tonight." I shot a glare at Rachel for telling him.

Bob led us through Ephesians 4:

> *...put off your old self, which is being corrupted by its deceitful desires, to be made new in attitude of your minds; and to put on the new self, created to be like God in true righteousness and holiness. (v.22-24)*

This was definitely something I wanted. I wanted a new self, but a piece of me was not willing to do whatever it took to get it. It was that control issue I still held on to. Bob stopped and commented to the group, "Usually people are on the floor by now by the power of the Spirit. God must be working on someone's heart." In an instant, my heart began to pound. I lowered my head, trying to hide as if people knew he was talking about me! God was meeting me where I was, and He knew I wasn't quite ready.

We divided into small groups to pray and Bob came over to me, Rachel, and another girl with us. He began by saying, "Which one of you has a Swedish mom?" Instantly my stomach dropped, and I got nervous thinking, *how does this guy know this stuff?*

I responded with a tremble in my voice, "Me."

He proceeded to say my mom would hold Jesus meetings in her home one day. In my head, I immediately began thinking about my dad. *How could this be possible? Dad is not a believer and he is very particular about his home. How would he allow this to go on?* Sitting on the floor in that living room, I felt small, exposed, as if my heart was being ripped open! Tears welled up in my eyes and I began to cry. What was happening?

Bob looked at me and said, "Nikki, you are a pastor, not a pastor in front of people, but among people, shepherding them, encouraging them. You have walls you have built up. Walls of lies you have told yourself, that others have told you, that Satan has told you. You need to break down those walls."

My heart felt as though it was ripping open even more. Now he was talking about *me*. About a piece of me I had closed up to the world. My weeping increased to a cry where I slouched over, my shoulders shaking. I can't explain it, but I felt as though some of those walls were breaking down in that moment. He was speaking directly to my soul! Bob concluded by saying, "Nikki, you will experience a deep joy. The Bible says joy comes in the morning. You will experience that joy." A pile of tears covered me when he finished.

Was this the power of the Holy Spirit? Was this the beginning of what my life would be like? Is this what releasing control looks like and not caring what others thought of me? I felt safe in this space, because this power was welcomed. In that moment, I did not care what others thought of me, something I held on to so tightly before. In that moment, God was trying to tell me something. Trying to get my attention through a man I had never met before.

I left the Bible study at 2 am, remnants of tears still in my eyes and on my face. I left awestruck and shaking my head in response to what happened, and occasionally laugh out of complete wonderment and curiosity. What the heck just happened? I rushed home and wrote every single thing down. I needed to document this moment, so I could refer back to it just to give me reassurance that I wasn't crazy!

I was astounded by this man whom I had never met before. He said words that penetrated the depths of my soul. Words from someone who knew the deepest parts of me. After some reflection, the explanation I kept going back to was, it had to be God!

The next day, as Bob said, I experienced a deep joy like I had never experienced before. I have always been a joyful, positive person, but this was different. I would laugh randomly, I felt warm inside, and the biggest smile covered my face. Something was different. I had been awakened to the Holy Spirit inside of me.

I went to church with my mom, and during the praise and singing portion of the worship service, I stretched my arms high above me. I felt as though a bright light was shining down from heaven on me. I felt warm, weightless, and peaceful. I thought, this must be what it feels like to be in the presence of Jesus!

After church, I shared with my mom what happened the night before. As I shared, I noticed tears well in her eyes. We pulled into our driveway and as we sat in the car, she pulled out a piece of paper from her Bible and asked me, "Have I ever shared this with you? This is a prophecy given to me in 1985." I shook my head. As she began reading, my eyes grew big and my eyebrows raised.

Her prophecy stated she would have Jesus meetings in her home, and her husband would come to know the Lord. When she finished reading, we looked at each other, eyes wide, then looked in the garage to see Dad standing at his workbench.

I said, "That stubborn man right there will know the Lord one day?!" By now, we both had smiles on our faces and eyes filled with tears in amazement as to what God was doing! A prophecy told to my mom twenty-seven years prior was repeated to me by a complete stranger!

My joy didn't end there. Two months after the first Bible

study, I went back.[4] But it wasn't as easy as it sounds. When Rachel invited me a second time, I refused at first. A piece of me was still fearful of the power of the Holy Spirit. If He did what He did the first time, what more could He do? I had given Him most of the control; that was enough. I wanted to hold on to a piece, just in case. I had convinced myself life was good. I was experiencing the joy of the Lord, I felt his presence wherever I went, what else could I possibly need? Boy, was I wrong!

I decided to go back anyway. While at the Bible study, Rachel and Bob's wife, Iliana, took me into a separate room in the house, away from the rest of the group, to pray for me. I sat on a bed in between them and they began praying as they laid hands on me. Iliana was on my right praying in tongues, and Rachel was on my left praying words I could understand. At the time, I didn't think much of it because I felt the warmth, light, and peace I had felt before. We were in the presence of the Holy Spirit and I was surrounded by people I trusted.

Suddenly, they both stopped, and Iliana said, "God wants me to touch your nose and tell you to stop taking life so seriously." This was something I had heard before. As they continued to pray, Iliana declared Proverbs 3:5-6. That's my favorite verse! She didn't know that. All of this was getting my attention because it was specific to me. I knew the Holy Spirit must have been present in that moment. Iliana stopped again and said, "Nikki, you need to surrender all you have to God."

I looked at her briefly. *I thought I did!* But then I remembered the piece I was still holding on to. That was the piece He wanted me to surrender. In that moment I thought,

4   October 2012

what do I have to lose? I desire to live a life for Jesus. I want to experience and understand God more. This may be the time to do it! I said aloud, "God, I surrender everything to you." Immediately, I felt a warm sensation within me from the top of my head to the bottom of my feet, and I began rocking back and forth in laughter.

This was the power of the Holy Spirit.

By surrendering every piece of my life, by letting go of control, I gave Him permission. I gave Him permission to do what He wanted, which was more than I could have ever imagined.

When they finished praying, my laughter continued, and I couldn't stop moving. I heard Rachel and Iliana speak to each other in agreement that I needed to go into the other room where another girl was cultivating the Holy Spirit. Rachel and I linked arms, as I was still letting out giggles, and entered the other room. Immediately both of our bodies jerked forward as though we were bowing.

There was an unexplainable power in this room, a power our human bodies couldn't handle. Rachel simply touched the girl's hand, and I dropped straight to the floor as if someone had pulled my legs out from under me. Once on the floor, I rolled back and forth, laughing so hard my cheeks hurt, my abs were sore, and my eyes blurred with tears. Rachel looked down at me and asked, "Can you believe this is happening to you?"

With a shortness of breath I replied, "No I can't!"

I remained this way for hours. Literally. I rolled around on the floor, laughing and being filled with the joy of the Lord. This kind of joy is unlike anything I have ever experienced. It's a joy that filled every part of my being. I felt completely consumed by this joy. It was a sense of carelessness, a sense of peace, a sense of weightlessness, a sense of enjoyment, and a sense of pleasure. The walls I once built up to shield myself from the ways of the Holy Spirit when I was in seventh grade had disappeared. I'd discovered freedom.

I was able to experience the Holy Spirit because I let go of the fear of losing control, the fear of rejection, the fear of what it means to be the perfect Christian. None of it mattered in that moment. All that mattered was I was in the presence of the Holy Spirit, and He was consuming every part of my being.

Bob walked over to me, leaned down, and said, "God wants you to share this joy with others. Keep some for yourself, but share with others." From that night on, I have been on a mission to share the joy the Holy Spirit has given me. And I keep going back to Him for more!

Chapter 7

Say Yes

I graduated from college with a major in Kinesiology/ Athletic Training.[5] After graduating, I felt the next step was to attend graduate school and get my Doctorate in Physical Therapy. I spent the next three years preparing. When it came time to apply to schools, I didn't know if I was following my heart or just going through the motions. I thought to myself, *I've gone this far, I might as well keep going.*

Deep in my heart, I knew something wasn't right. I began to pray, "God, if you want me to go to graduate school please make it so clear. Close doors and open others." I continued with the applications and applied to six different graduate schools. With much anticipation, I waited for a response, only to find out I was not accepted. Not only that, two of the schools lost my paperwork. If that's not a clear sign, I don't know what is. Deep down I felt a sense of relief, until the *Now what?* question popped into my head.

Shortly after learning I would not be attending graduate school, Rachel sent me a text that simply read, "Look up the

5   Point Loma Nazarene University 2010

World Race." Out of curiosity, I did. I googled "The World Race" and what I found were videos and blogs of people traveling the world for Jesus.[6] Two of my favorite things! The more I read about this organization, the more I thought about the possibility. Eleven months in eleven different countries, carrying all your belongings in a backpack. This was right up my alley! But doubt crept in my mind, and I began thinking, *eleven months is so long! I've never been away from home that long, and to be in so many different countries and cultures? How am I going to pay for this?*

I tried to avoid the pull I felt to go on this adventure, yet more and more people came into my life who knew about the World Race. Where were these people years ago? I couldn't get the World Race out of my head; I thought about it daily. Throughout my research, a certain time of year and route stood out to me from the rest: *January 2014, Route 3.* Three times a year, five squads (groups of forty to fifty people) are sent on various country routes around the world. For some reason, that specific route jumped out at me. It started in Central America, jumped over to Southeast Asia, and ended in Africa.

I couldn't run from this idea, so I deepened my research and connected with an acquaintance who had gone on the Race. She shared some of her stories from her experience and her heart with me, and I shared my heart with her. We talked for nearly an hour when she concluded with, "Nikki, you need to go."

I continued wrestling with the idea until I did the noncommittal thing and applied "just to see what would happen." I was curious but not fully committed. I had a phone interview, and was told I would hear back from them within

---

6   theworldrace.org

two weeks. However, less than one week later, I got a phone call from the organization saying I had been accepted and they would be more than happy to have me as part of Route 3, leaving January 2014. All I needed to do in that moment to secure my place was to give a deposit, which I did on the spot.

I hung up the phone and stood frozen in my room. I was stunned.

What did I just do? What did I just sign myself up for? Did I really just send my deposit? I had no idea what I was getting myself into, but I know the Holy Spirit was with me every step of the way. He continued to bring people into my life who had either gone on the Race or knew someone who did. I met every single financial deadline. People from all walks of my life donated to this experience. My dad, who didn't want me to go, eventually got on board and asked many of his business associates to donate. He even sold his Sea Doo and put the money toward my trip.

This experience taught me God will use the people you'd never expect. I am grateful and humbled by the generous people in my life. If you donated to my World Race experience, I am forever grateful to you. And if it wasn't for you, I probably wouldn't be writing this book!

In January of 2014, I departed with my squad to our first country, Guatemala. We traveled country to country, spending a month in each one, partnering with different ministries throughout. The squad was split into teams of six to seven people and assigned to ministries across each country. These ministries varied from working with the elderly, construction, providing day care, going into bars in Red Light districts and talking with bar girls, living at an orphanage, working and living in a blind community, and leading Bible studies or church services. You name it, we most likely did it.[7]

I said yes to an opportunity God placed in front of me. Many times during these eleven months I thought to myself, *I could be sitting in a classroom right now but instead I'm in (name a country).* I gained a global perspective, and throughout this book I will share stories with you from this epic year of my life. This was not only an unforgettable trip, it was a catalyst for where I am in my life now. Writing this book has helped me process my experiences. It has been five years since I went on the World Race, and I am still processing it. I believe this is something I will do for the rest of my life. The Holy Spirit showed up during that year in ways I had never experienced for myself, but had only read about in the Bible or heard stories from other people. God stirred my faith, and in the following chapters I will share some of those moments with you.

7   nikkiromani.theworldrace.org

Chapter 8

Who is the Holy Spirit?

But the Counselor, the Holy Spirit, whom the Father will send in my name, will teach you all things and will remind you of everything I have said to you.

John 14:26

Before we get into all the crazy, incredible ways I have experienced the Holy Spirit, let's discuss who He is. Billy Graham, who was considered to be the world's greatest evangelist said, "The Holy Spirit is not an impersonal force, like gravity or magnetism, He is a person with all the attributes of personality. But not only is He a person; He is divine as well... He comforts us. Guides us. Sanctifies us. He tells His servants what to preach. He directs missionaries where to go. He helps us in our infirmities."[8]

---

8   *Who is the Holy Spirit* by Billy Graham

In Francis Chan's book *Forgotten God*, he lays out who the Spirit is and I think it is a great overview of the Holy Spirit.[9]

The Spirit...

- Gives us words to say when we don't know what to say during hardship and trials. He teaches us how to defend ourselves.
(Mark 13:11; Luke 12:12)
- Leads and instructs us where to go. He is our guide, counselor,and leads us in truth. (Psalm 143:10; John 16:13)
- Gives us power. (Acts 1:8)
- Sets us free from sin and death. (Romans 8:2)
- Adopts us into God's family as His children and co-heirs with Christ. (Romans 8:15-17)
- Convicts us of the guilt from sin. (John 16:8)
- Gives us hope. (Romans 15:13)
- Gives us the ability to release the gifts He has given us (manifestations, for example). (1 Corinthians 12:7)
- Gives us His fruits. (Gal 5:22-23)
- Knows the depths of God, and therefore, gives us wisdom from God. (1 Corinthians 2:10-12; John 16:13)

The Holy Spirit is Counselor, Guide, and Confidant. He is the tug we feel, the conviction deep within us. He is the One we follow through the journey of life. We are called to live a spirit-filled life. Think of it like the wind in a sail. The sailboat goes wherever the wind leads, so too should your life with the Holy Spirit.

Before Jesus' death on the cross, He shared with the disciples how He had to go in order for the "counselor" to

9   *Forgotten God* by Francis Chan

come, who is the Spirit of truth and will guide in truth.[10] After the resurrection of Jesus, He appeared to His disciples and breathed on them to receive the Holy Spirit.[11]

When Jesus ascended into Heaven after His resurrection, the disciples were told to stay in Jerusalem for the gift from the Father, who is the Comforter, and they would be baptized with the Holy Spirit.[12] Like a violent wind from heaven the house was filled with the Holy Spirit to whom each one was filled.[13] The Holy Spirit is a gift from God which will never be taken away, but it's our job to use what we have been given.[14]

Looking back on my life, I now realize all those times the Holy Spirit was nudging me and talking to me. I just didn't know it was Him or understand until I decided to pursue a relationship with Him. Relationships take time, but you've got to start somewhere, and the Holy Spirit is eager to have one with you. He wants you to experience more, but first you must be a good steward with what He has already given. Once you steward well what you have, more will be given.

I have grown up hearing about the Trinity; the Father, Son, and Holy Spirit being One. However, the Father and Son were the two most talked about. I didn't know much about the Holy Spirit and the role He played. Thinking of God, Jesus, and the Holy Spirit as One can be difficult to comprehend, especially since we often overcomplicate things. We will never fully understand all God is, and I believe that's the point. We must rely on Him because of this, and that is God's intention. I

10 Matthew 16:5-7,13 11

11 John 20:22

12 Acts 1:4-5

13 Acts 2:2-4

14 1 John 3:24

also believe if He did tell us everything, we would become overwhelmed.

For instance, I have prayed, "break my heart, for what breaks yours." When He has answered with a fraction of what breaks His heart, I am crippled by the weight on my chest. My heart feels like it's breaking, seeing His hurting children around me.

When you experience something like this you will understand why He shares what He shares when He shares it. You will begin to understand God, His Spirit, and His heart for you and His children. Spending time and sitting in His presence will help you understand Him a little more each time. Mark Batterson says, "The more people grow spiritually, the more prophetic they become."[15] The more in tune with God's voice and aligned with His Spirit, the more we will begin to understand. However, just when you think you know the ways of God, He will surprise you. He is unpredictable, but He always has your best in mind.

---

15 *Whisper: How to Hear the Voice of God* by Mark Batterson

Chapter 9

To Be Baptized

I baptize you with water for repentance. But after me will come one who is more powerful than I, whose sandals I am not fit to carry. He will baptize you with the Holy Spirit and with fire.

Matthew 3:11

When I was ten years old, I was baptized with water by my pastor in the sanctuary of our church. This was my public declaration of repentance, my salvation, my love for Jesus, and my desire to follow Him all the days of my life.[16]

At the age of twenty-four, I was baptized with the Holy Spirit.[17] To be baptized in the Holy Spirit is a different kind of submersion. When you are baptized with water, you are submerged below the surface of the water. When you are baptized in the Spirit, it is so powerful it's hard to stay upright.

16 Pasadena First Church of the Nazarene

17 Azusa Pacific University Bible Study with Bob and Iliana

Everyone may experience this in a different way; nonetheless, I want to share with you what I felt.

When I was sitting on the bed in between Rachel and Iliana who were praying over me, I cried out to God, "I surrender everything to you!" I consider this the permission slip, and within milliseconds, I felt a warm sensation surge throughout my body, starting at my head and moving all the way through my body down to my toes. With my eyes closed, I began rocking back and forth, laughing. I was in a state of surrender, so I was not about to stop what was happening. I released control of my body, and in this state of full surrender, I felt a power like no other. My body couldn't stay upright, and I hit the floor and rolled around.

When the disciples were filled with the Holy Spirit, He came in like a "violent wind."[18] Baptism of the Spirit is not delicate by any means. However, the disciples were eager and ready for the Spirit to come. They, too, were in a state of full surrender. Full surrender, I believe, is the key point to my experience, or anyone else's for that matter.

You cannot force it and you have the free will to stop it. But if you want the fullness of God and His Spirit, you have to let go of control and let it happen as it will. It is unlike anything I have ever experienced. You must experience it for yourself, which is one of the reasons I am writing this book—to encourage you to experience the Holy Spirit in your own way. Start by surrendering. You may not fall on your back as I did. You may not experience holy laughter as I did. However, you will know you are under the influence of the Spirit when your body does whatever He tells it to. It's radical and completely worth it. You feel closer to God on a much deeper level.

---

18 Acts 2:2

When you invite Jesus into your life, He gives you His spirit. From the time you receive salvation, the Holy Spirit is within you, but there is something that happens when you are baptized in the Spirit. It's as though you are on another level of connection with Him and He draws you closer. Like being baptized with water as a declaration, and getting rid of your old self, being baptized with the Holy Spirit is another declaration of you surrendering your life to Him.

This is not something that has to happen in order for you to be a Christian. I believe, however, this is something we should experience and something God wants us to experience to be closer to Him and fulfill our purpose on this earth. "On earth as it is in heaven" (Matthew 6:10b). We are to be the vessels of bringing heaven to earth, and we do that with the Holy Spirit.

Almost two years after my own baptism of the Holy Spirit, God used me to baptize others in the Spirit, and has continued to pour His Spirit in and upon me.[19]

During our fifth month on the World Race, we were in Thailand for debrief. Our squad of forty-three members were all together at this time. One night, we were in a banquet hall at a hotel and our spiritual father and coach Gary was sharing his wisdom with us. He is a wise man, in tune with the Holy Spirit and His movement. As Gary stood in front of us, speaking, he bent over, laughing.

As he laughed, he told us this had never happened to him before in front of a large group. In that moment I knew the Spirit was on the move and moving toward me, because I had an open heart to receive. Sure enough, I was slowing being pulled from my chair as my body felt heavier and heavier,

19 On the World Race in Thailand 2014

and I ended up face down on the floor. After five months with the squad, they knew the effect the Spirit had on me, so it was no surprise to them. I heard someone say, "There goes Nikki."

While I lie on the floor, I couldn't lift my head or push myself up. I heard God say to me, "Stay here. I am filling you up." I didn't know what was going on or the plan God had, but when He wants to fill you up, you do not refuse. I was on the floor the entire time Gary was speaking and would experience surges of laughter and moments of peace. As Gary finished, he said, "I feel the move of the Holy Spirit and He wants to baptize you. Let's have the leaders go around and pray for those who want to be baptized in the Holy Spirit." Immediately the weight lifted, and God so clearly stated, "Get up. Now is the time." I cannot begin to tell you how full I felt, how connected to the Holy Spirit I was.

I walked around the room with Gary and my fellow squad leaders, Erica and David. Gary asked my squad mates one by one if they believed in Jesus and what He had done for them, and asked for permission to be baptized in the Holy Spirit. When I placed my hand on the individual, I knew deep down what their answer was and would declare, "Yes! Yes, they do!" The person would answer, and we prayed over them.

I was so full of the Spirit that as we prayed for each person, I would lay hands on them and start shaking my head back and forth. Picture the music video for Willow Smith's "Whip my Hair." That's what it looked like! Seriously, if you watch the music video, you'll see her whipping her braids, and that's what my ponytail looked like.

As the Spirit moved, laughter filled the atmosphere. He was on the move and people were falling on the floor because the power of the Spirit was so great, their human bodies could not handle it. It was not forced. We did not push them. The

Holy Spirit was invited by each individual and would fall back, and of course, we would catch them. This continued for about two hours.

After praying for everyone, our squad momma and coach Joey came over to me. She placed her hands on my head and said, "It's your turn. I pray your head is so heavy you fall on the ground and do not get up until God is done filling you up." With my head in between her hands, she guided me to the floor. My head felt like a heavy weight. I don't know how long I stayed there, but I again experienced surges of laughter and of peace. I just closed my eyes and took in the aroma in the air, heard the laughter, and sensed the joy and freedom in the room. It was beautiful!

God does not leave us dry. The only and best way for us to minister to others is if we come from a place of fullness. God filled me up before and after He used me to pray over His children. He knows we cannot do this out of our own strength, so He must fill us up with His strength and with His Spirit. I would have never been able to do what I did out of my own strength, but I was willing and God used me to touch His children in a new way that night, and to be filled with the Holy Spirit on another level.

This was a night I will never forget! When I think of being baptized in the Holy Spirit, I picture what this night was like; the senses, the sounds, the rejoicing, the tears of joy, the shouts to Jesus, the love that filled the room. It was not forced on anyone, but was contagious. When you see someone receive the Holy Spirit in this way, it's hard not to want more of Him for yourself. One of my squad mates was watching me whip my ponytail around and shake as I touched our other squad mates. She laughed, "I can't help but laugh at what I'm seeing. God is so funny and it's contagious."

God really does have a sense of humor and likes to have fun. I sure had fun that night as people experienced God in new and fresh ways, but it was because they were willing. They had a deep desire and wanted to experience the Holy Spirit.

We as Christians not only have the opportunity to be baptized with water as a sign of repentance and salvation, but also of the Holy Spirit and fire. Holy Spirit baptism is not a one and done kind of deal. Daily we should be filled with the Spirit. Imagine a world filled with people who use the access we have to the Holy Spirit. Lives would be changed forever!

Peter and John are examples of what it looks like to be filled with the Spirit and go back for more. In Acts 2, these men, along with the other disciples, receive the Holy Spirit. In Acts 3, Peter and John use the power they have just received through the baptism of the Spirit to heal a lame man who was unable to walk. In Acts 4, Peter and John go back to their friends and ask God for more of the Holy Spirit, more boldness even after they had just witnessed the miracle of a lame man walking.

If I want to be more like Jesus, I need to surrender and allow the Holy Spirit to consume me and show me the ways of God, and I need to do this daily. When I think of my days on mission trips in other countries and how I witnessed miracles, healings, and deliverance in others, I think of the state of mind I had. I was completely reliant on the Holy Spirit. I was open to whatever He had in store for each day and surrendered every day to Him while on the field. It is my job, as well as yours, to rely on the Holy Spirit on a day-to-day basis.

Chapter 10

The Power of Spiritual Gifts

There are different kinds of gifts, but the same Spirit. There are different kinds of service but the same Lord. There are different kinds of working, but the same God works all of them in all men. Now to each one the manifestation of the spirit is given for the common good.

1 Corinthians 12:4-7

It starts with faith. Faith is confidence in what we hope for and assurance in what we do not see.[20] It's living out your life in the natural to create change in the supernatural. I love Hebrews 11, which is known as the "Hall of Faith." This chapter lists for us the people who lived by faith, because without faith it is impossible to please God. God rewards those who have faith and earnestly seek Him.

20 Hebrews 11:1

In order to receive any of the gifts the Holy Spirit wants to give to us, we must have faith that He exists, and live a life of evidence of this belief. If you do not have faith, you will not believe you have the ability to receive the gifts of the Spirit and the workings of the supernatural. Do you have faith? All you need is faith as small as a mustard seed (Luke 17:6). You need to open your eyes and heart to the impossible.

There are many stories throughout this book of miracles, because someone had faith the impossible would happen. My faith was small when I experienced my first miracle, but when it happened, my faith grew more. With each small act of faith, it grows more and more. We can't see God, but we have faith He is with us. We can't see the Holy Spirit, but we can feel His presence around us.

Spiritual gifts are of the supernatural and are given by the prompting of the Holy Spirit. "All these [spiritual gifts] are the work of one and the same Spirit, and he gives them to each one, just as He determines."[21] These gifts are given with the purpose of building up the church (I don't mean a physical building. I'm referring to the body of Christ) and expanding the kingdom of God (1 Corinthians 14:12). Once the Holy Spirit gives you a gift, He will never take it away.

Each one of us has gifts according to the grace given to us (Romans 12:6). You will learn what gifts you possess when you remain in the presence of God. I believe the more you are walking with and remaining in Jesus, the more gifts will be released upon you. Like Jesus says in John 15, if we remain in Him we will produce fruit. God loves us and He wants us to have supernatural power to bring glory to His name and to be a witness to unbelievers and encouragement to believers. He has given us all the authority in heaven and

21 1 Corinthians 12:11

on earth. And that authority needs to be unleashed! Why are we not using what has been given to us? Are we afraid? Do we not realize the power that is within us? I believe most of us don't know the power and authority we carry. Living a life with the Holy Spirit is living a life of faith.

I believe the more we give of ourselves to God, the more He will give to us. I am learning the gifts of the spirit come with time and when we walk in daily obedience. There are a variety of different gifts of the spirit and they are all from the same spirit, the same God (Ephesians 4:11; 1 Peter 4:10–11).

One gift is not superior to another. They are all needed in the body of Christ. Not everyone will receive the same gifts. This is laid out for us by Paul in 1 Corinthians. Do not compare your gifts to those around you. We are all unique, and even if some of us have the same spiritual gift, such as tongues, each person's spiritual language will sound different. Just like our personalities are unique, our spiritual gifts are unique and compliment us. Do you have the same laugh as another person? Just as your laugh is unique, your giftings are unique.

Before I share with you some of the gifts, keep this in mind, "For God is not a God of disorder but of peace."[22] We must be responsible with these gifts. There is a time and place and I pray God gives you discernment. God desires order in His church, however He is not to be put in a box. Structure is good, but be flexible and allow for times like extended worship or prayer or whatever the Spirit is leading you to do. You will forever be changed when you invite the Holy Spirit to move.

I want to share the spiritual gifts I have experienced. Not everyone experiences them in this way, and not everyone

22   1 Corinthians 14:33

has these gifts. These are my stories, and I want to encourage you to ask the Holy Spirit what your gifts are. Seek God and He will reveal them to you when you are ready.

Speaking In Tongues

...to another speaking in different kinds of tongues, and still another the interpretation of tongues...

1 Corinthians 12:10

I was lying on the floor in Thailand in the presence of the Holy Spirit. God had just used me to baptize others in the Holy Spirit and then He flattened me on my back. As I lie there listening to the sounds of the room, I thanked God for using me in the way He did. And that's when it happened— unfamiliar words came out of my mouth. This occurred after I had obeyed God by praying over His children and showing them a God they had never met, introducing them to the Holy Spirit in a new way. Then God gave me a gift, the gift of tongues. I wasn't speaking loudly; no one else could hear me. I was having a conversation with God in a different language. It was a precious moment between me and my heavenly Father.

Speaking in tongues was something that once terrified me, I didn't want to have anything to do with it. I heard people speaking in tongues in a disordered way, and I know this happens a lot in the church. People will speak out loud in different tongues, when it should be a precious moment between you and God speaking with Him in a heavenly language. Only, and *only* if there is someone to interpret, should you speak louder. This is clearly stated in the Bible and we need to obey and not scare people away.[23]

I know I am not the only one who was turned away from the ways of the Spirit because of people making a scene. These gifts should not be used to edify yourself, but used to glorify God and edify the church. Too many people abuse the gifts and do not use them properly to build up the body of Christ. Here is what Paul says about speaking in tongues:

> *For anyone who speaks in a tongue does not speak to men but to God...He who speaks in a tongue edifies himself, but he who prophesies edifies the church...Unless you speak intelligible words with your tongue, how will anyone know what you are saying? You will just be speaking into the air. Undoubtedly there are all sorts of languages in the world, yet none of them is without meaning. If then I do not grasp the meaning of what someone is saying, I am a foreigner to the speaker, and he is a foreigner to me...For this reason anyone who speaks in a tongue should pray that he may interpret what he says.*

1 Corinthians 14:2, 4

I experienced an orderly way of someone speaking in tongues. It was that night sitting on the bed in between Rachel and Iliana. Iliana on my right prayed in tongues while Rachel, on my left, prayed in English. In that moment, I felt as though one was interpreting what the other was praying. I don't

23 1 Corinthians 14:28

necessarily know if this was the case, but in the moment I felt safe and knew the Holy Spirit was present. I was not afraid of the unfamiliar language because it came from a trusted source, and because someone else prayed in my native language.

> *If anyone speaks in a tongue, two- or at the most three- should speak, one at a time, and someone must interpret. If there is no interpreter, the speaker should keep quiet in the church and speak to himself and God. Be eager to speak in prophecy, and do not forbid speaking in tongues. But everything should be done in a fitting and orderly way.*

1 Corinthians 14:27-28

One and a half billion people identify with speaking in tongues. They come from every country and denomination. In fact, seventy-five million are part of the Roman Catholic Church. To some, speaking in tongues seems "unorthodox," but this is the way Jesus lived in the Jewish culture.[24] And as Christians we strive to live as Jesus did, right?

A friend of mine and her mom both speak in tongues. Once when we were all together, they told me to start saying random words and make up sounds and it would happen. Deep in my spirit I knew it wouldn't. This experience can't be forced. I felt God telling me it would happen, but not yet.

The gift of tongues is received through the baptism by the Holy Spirit. For some this may happen right away, like it does in Acts 2:4, 10:46, and 19:6. For me this wasn't the case.

24 "Praying in the Spirit" by Jimmy Swaggart
https://www.cmalliance.org/about/beliefs/perspectives/spiritual-gifts

People receive different gifts of the Spirit at different times. And speaking in tongues was something I received one year after my first Holy Spirit baptism.

Think of it like a secret language between you and God. A language that cannot be written down or repeated. A language Satan does not understand. A language so powerful it directly connects you to heaven. A language excluding ulterior motives. A language for prayer when we do not have the words. Speaking in tongues is like an immediate ushering into God's presence.

Intercession

While in Thailand on the World Race, half of our group went to the red-light district, while the other half stayed back to intercede on their behalf. The red-light district is like entering a war zone. It is full of darkness, bondage, and slavery. Stepping on those streets, I felt the weight of evil upon me. However, knowing I had people praying on my behalf, this weight seemed a little bit lighter. I felt protected.

Walking along those streets, hearing the music blaring from the bars, seeing the flashing neon lights, looking up to see women trapped in window boxes, dancing to draw in customers, I knew evil was present, but there was a power of something greater because I carried it along with those I was with. The half of the group who stayed back to pray, started praying when our group left and didn't stop until we returned. Once the groups were back together at the end of the night, we would debrief and share our encounters. People who were on the streets said they felt a pull to go into a certain bar or talk to a certain person, and come to find there was someone on the other end praying for that exact thing to happen! It was pretty spectacular and made us realize we serve a big

God and learned the power of intercession.

I was reading through an article I found in my grandma's belongings. The author wrote, "Authoritative intercessors are men and women whose eyes have been opened to the full knowledge of their place in Christ." He goes on to say these intercessors view the Word of God like a battle plan against the enemy to defend the kingdom of God.[25] God wants to partner with us to advance His kingdom, and intercession is one way to fight and through these prayers God will fulfill His promises.

I like the analogy of using the Bible as a strategic battle plan. Like Paul says in Ephesians, our fight is not against flesh and blood.[26] We need intercessors and prayer warriors to pray in the spirit for our victory! We need to pray like it depends on God, and work like it depends on us.

In Greek, *intercession* is used as a way of approaching a King for a favor. As God is our King, we need to come to Him with our requests through the act of surrender. Getting on our knees is a great position for surrender and shows humility.

Intercession can be used for the repentance of a person or people group, as Moses demonstrated. Moses interceded for the people of Israel and for his brother Aaron. He lie flat on his back and did not eat or drink for forty days and forty nights, pleading with the Lord not to destroy them for the sin they had committed. In this position of surrender, the Lord listened to him.[27]

Sometimes, God will bring a person to the forefront of my mind. At first, I didn't know what to think when this happened, but now I view this as God telling me to pray and

25 "The Authority of the Intercessor" Rev. J. A. MacMillan

26 Ephesians 6:12

27 Deuteronomy 9:19

intercede on their behalf. Most times I have no idea what to pray, and that's ok. The Holy Spirit will intercede. The next time a person pops into your head, whoever they may be, pray for them! You may be stepping into a battle you cannot see on their behalf.

We have authority in the name of Jesus because His spirit is within us. Use the authority given to you. Rev. J. A. MacMillan says, "The church needs intercessors who have learned the secret of taking hold of the power of God and directing it against the strategic advances of the enemy."[28]

A friend of mine mentioned she felt God wanted to give her the gift of intercession. At first, she didn't want it. She thought back to the times she had prayed for someone and remembered how exhausting it was. She was deliberately praying a fighting prayer. I told her intercession does not always look like this.

There are times God will bring someone to mind, you say a prayer for them, and move on. Sometimes there is more to it and you have to pray a fighting prayer for them, get on your knees, and be at war in the Spirit. And yes, that can be exhausting! But think of the life you are praying for. It's not about you and how you feel, it's about listening to the Holy Spirit's prompting and using the power of prayer. Our mission is to advance the kingdom of God.

The Holy Spirit is an intercessor and intercedes on our behalf. He alone can interpret the needs of the human heart. He intercedes for us while we are on the earth. You don't even need to say actual words, like it says in Romans 8:26-27,

> *... the Spirit himself intercedes for us with groans*
> *that words cannot express. And he who searches*

28 "The Authority of the Intercessor" Rev. J. A. MacMillan

our hearts knows the mind of the Spirit, because
the Spirit intercedes for the saints in accordance
to God's will.

Jesus intercedes for us in Heaven. Like it says in Hebrews 7:25,

He is able to save completely those who come
to God through him, because he always lives to
intercede for them.

Prophecy

...to another prophecy...

1 Corinthians 12:10

Even my servants, both men and women, I will
pour out my Spirit in those days, And they will
prophesy.

Acts 2:18

The word *prophecy* means, "foretelling or predicting what is to come; a divinely inspired revelation".[29] A prophetic word is "strengthening, encouraging, and comforting."[30] Prophecy is a precious gift given to edify the church.[31]

Prophecy can occur in the form of dreams, visions, God speaking to you directly, or God sharing through another person. I shared with you about Bob who told me specific details only God would know about my life. That was

29 dictionary.com

30 1 Corinthians 14:3

31 1 Corinthians 14:4

prophecy. I didn't know Bob, and yet he was speaking into a detail of my life not many people know about. I knew in that moment the words were from God and I felt strengthened, encouraged, and comforted.

Banning Liebscher from Jesus Culture said, "The prophetic is confirmation that what was heard from God was correct, or faith building."[32] It ignites faith and gives you hope for what is to come. Prophecy can be a warning as to what's coming, but also gives hope of prosperity. The Israelites were promised a land flowing with milk and honey; however, for the three days following this prophecy, they didn't even have water. They were in a struggle, yet had the hope they would receive what God had promised.

Sometimes God gives us prophecies we have to wait decades to see fulfilled. Nevertheless, during those years leading up to the fulfillment we are being equipped for what is to come. I think of a vision I had speaking on stage to hundreds of people. I couldn't imagine myself being on stage at the time He gave this prophetic word to me. But it's the hope I hold onto and the glimpse into the future God has for me. This glimpse motivates and gives me determination to keep pressing forward until that promise is fulfilled.

I once heard Havilah Cunnington say, "Prophecy is like receiving a hug from God." This is so true! When I think of the times someone shared a word with me from God, I felt as though He was reaching down to give me a hug, letting me know everything would be ok, and that He sees me. He loves us and wants to share His plans with us. He is a good Father who wants to uplift us.

If you've never had anyone share a prophecy over you, it's as though someone is looking deep into your soul and

32 On Shawn Bolz podcast - Prophetic Living Episode

lifting you up from a place of unbelief. It strengthens your hope and belief in the one true God who knows you better than anyone ever could. It's mind blowing, but at the same time brings comfort and reassurance.

The gift of prophecy was something I practiced at training camp for the World Race. Half of our group stood in a circle while the other half stood in front of them, creating an inner circle. We were then encouraged to pray and ask the Holy Spirit for a word to share with the person in front of us. It could be anything. We just had to share. Let me tell you, it was nerve-wracking. Seriously, talk about stepping out of your comfort zone.

However, as a whole we extended grace toward one another. I remember standing face to face with someone I had never met before. I placed my hands on her and silently prayed, asking the Holy Spirit to reveal something to me about her. Before I said what I thought I heard from God, I gave a disclaimer that I had no idea if this meant anything to her, but I'd share it anyway. If anything, it was a nice encouragement. This act of listening for God's voice for someone else is something to be practiced. The more you do it, the clearer pictures or words you will receive for them, and the better you will be able to discern God's voice from your own. Prophecy is a gift all Christians should receive. Even Moses said, "I wish all the Lord's people were prophets and that the Lord would put his Spirit on them!"[33]

Another way to receive prophecy is through scriptures. While I was on the Race, my coach Gary prayed for me and spoke Deuteronomy 28:1-14 over my life. I grabbed my Bible and flipped to the passage. I was encouraged by what I read. It's a promise for not just me, but for all of us that if we obey God,

33 Numbers 11:29

we will be blessed, enemies will flee, we will have abundant prosperity, lending to many nations, and borrowing from none. As I read this passage, I felt as though God was giving me a hug. I felt seen and known by my Father in Heaven.

Pay attention to prophecy. Hold onto it and see it through, no matter how long it takes. This will sustain you through the trial and the storm. God is faithful, and He will fulfill the promises He has given you.

Wisdom

> *To one there is given through the Spirit the message of wisdom...*

> 1 Corinthians 12:8

Word of wisdom, according to Gladys Johnson (aka Grandma), is the "supernatural revelation by the Spirit of divine purpose. The supernatural unfolding of God's plans and purposes."[34] An example from the Bible is in Genesis 6:13-22, where God tells Noah He will bring a flood to the earth and instructs him to build an ark. God tells Noah what is going to happen, and in turn, Noah gains wisdom from God.

Shawn Bolz wrote a book titled *God Secrets*. In this book he says, "You can know the secrets of God and use that knowledge to transform the world around you."[35] We have access to God's thoughts and His wisdom, which can be used to touch people in a vulnerable way. I am a life coach, and when I am with a client listening to her and engaging with her, the Holy Spirit gives me the ability to "read between the

---

34 Gladys Johnson sermon notes "Gifts of the Spirit Lesson 2"

35 *God Secrets* by Shawn Bolz

lines" of what the client is actually saying. As a client talks, I can identify the deeper issue and sum up what they are not saying. This has happened on multiple occasions. One of my clients even commented on it. At one point she said, "That's exactly it! How did you know? It's as if you are reading between the lines of what I am saying."

All I could say was, "God." God gives me the wisdom in the moment to share with others. This is a gift. Wisdom, just like all the other gifts, comes with spending time with Jesus. The more time I spend with him on a regular basis, the more wisdom I feel I have because I am learning more about God and His Spirit. He shares things with me when I sit and listen.

If you want to read more about wisdom in the Bible, read through the book of Proverbs. This entire book gives us wise counsel. The author of Proverbs instructs us to trust in the Lord with all our hearts, commit to the Lord whatever we do and our plans will succeed, and warns us about the power of our words and having a cheerful heart. There are many wisdom nuggets in this book. With thirty-one chapters, you could read one chapter a day for one month. This is something I have done and will continue to do.

Healing

...to another gifts of healing by that one spirit...

1 Corinthians 12:9

I am still in the process of learning what my gifts are and how to use them, and I think I always will be. I sat with the Holy Spirit and asked Him to share my gifts with me. He gave me a list. Healing hands is on the list. I thought back to the time

I first discovered this gift, when God used me to heal my friend Christina's back (I share this story in the miracles chapter.).

Another time, I was praying with a friend and as I prayed for her, I placed my hand on her shoulder. I prayed for freedom and the release of fear over her life. After I finished praying, she shared how she felt a release from her and said I had healing hands. This is emotional healing. Healing can happen both physically and emotionally. Physical healing is a body part being restored, and an example of emotional healing is the release of fear over someone's life.

The Holy Spirit is inside of you, and whatever you carry can be transferred through you to the person you are touching and praying for in the name of Jesus. I have been on the other end of this, and when someone has prayed for me, I have felt the transfer of what they were carrying onto me. This is the act of the Holy Spirit.

Discerning of Spirits

...to another distinguishing between spirits...

1 Corinthians 12:10

Discerning of spirits can be represented in a couple different ways. I think of the time I sang praises to God, sensing the Holy Spirit, but aware of another spirit in the room. The difference was the feeling I had. The Holy Spirit was full of joy and peace. The other spirit was full of anxiety and heaviness. I also think of the times I have been confused about which voice was mine and which was God's. Moments of debate whether the Spirit of God was telling me to do something, or if it was the voice of another spirit.

When you are captured by the desire for love, these spirits and voices can be a bit confusing. Going back to that first, young relationship I was in, I thought for sure he was the one I would marry. However, something deep inside me was pulling me back, telling me it wasn't right. I was blinded by love, or what I thought was love at the ripe age of seventeen. Many signs pointed to no; nonetheless, I was convinced this would be the perfect situation. I was confusing God's voice with my own. I had convinced myself this was right, even though I knew it was wrong. That was the Holy Spirit convicting me.

Even though I was confused about which voice to listen to, God loved me enough to keep me safe. To do the thing I avoided. I believe the Holy Spirit broke up with my boyfriend for me. It's a crazy thought, and it's moments like these I look back on my life and realize the Holy Spirit has my best interests in mind. He is the Spirit we should follow, and no other.

If you are wondering how to discern these different spirits, spend time with God and He will show you. I repeat this truth throughout the book because it's important and fuels our relationship with Him.

In 1 John 4 we are warned about different spirits and are advised to test these spirits to know whether they are of God. This is because many false prophets inhabit the world along with many other spiritual forces. We are told in this scripture how to discern. Verse 4 tells us every spirit from God acknowledges that Jesus came in the flesh from God, but every spirit that does not acknowledge Jesus is not from God. This spirit will speak as the world speaks and the world will do as it says. Because we are of God, we are to listen to what He says.

In the book of John, we are told God's sheep know His voice and follow Him (John 10:27). If you spend time with the Good Shepherd, you will know His voice and be able to discern His voice from others. I talk more about how to discern the voice of God in a later chapter.

Ask the Holy Spirit what your gifts are. He will reveal them in due time. And when you are given these gifts, it's your responsibility to use them. Do not stow them away and hide them. Bring them out for others to see and experience! Be a good steward of your gifts and you will see fruit. With spiritual gifts come the fruits of the spirit: "love, joy, peace, patience, kindness, goodness, faithfulness, gentleness, and self- control" (Galatians 5:22-23). Create a space even now to do this. Set this book down for a moment and grab a pen and paper. Holy Spirit, come and share the gifts you have bestowed on this precious one.

The Five Fold Ministry

> *Christ himself gave the apostles, the prophets, the evangelists, the pastors and teachers, to equip his people for works of service, so that the body of Christ may be built up until we all reach unity in the faith and in the knowledge of the Son of God and become mature, attaining to the whole measure of the fullness of Christ.*

Ephesians 4:11-13

Along with the gifts listed in 1 Corinthians, which we are not limited to by any means, additional gifts are given on account of the Holy Spirit, "The 5-Fold Ministry."[36] This includes apostles, prophets, evangelists, pastors, and teachers.

36   1 Corinthians 12:27-31

This structure of ministry is used throughout both the Old and New Testaments.

Apostle

Apostles build the foundation of the church with sound doctrine and Christ as the core (Ephesians 2:20). Apostles commonly move in the giftings of healing, faith, miracles, words of wisdom, discerning of spirits, and prophecy.[37] Paul was an apostle of Jesus.

Prophet

The description of a prophet is given to us in Deuteronomy 18. Prophets will speak the words God has given them (also known as *prophecy*). Prophets have the ability to recognize the gifts of an individual and call them out into their position of ministry in the church. Prophets found in the Bible are Isaiah, Daniel, and John the Baptist.

Evangelist

Evangelists are those who are a part of the outreach for the church. They go into communities around the world to share the love and good news of Jesus. An example of an evangelist of our time was Billy Graham. He was a man who traveled to many countries, speaking in front of thousands to one million people sharing the simple gospel. He didn't stay in one place for long, he was on the move spreading the name of Jesus.

Pastor

Pastors are committed to their people. Unlike the evangelist who travels, the pastor stays with the church, committed to

37 https://www.generals.org/articles/single/do-you-know-why-fivefold-ministry-is- essential/ by Diane Lake church.

walking alongside their people. They are the shepherds of the flock and speak the truth of God's Word. I have been told I am a pastor among people, encouraging them and walking alongside them.

An example of a pastor in my life was my grandma. She was a pastor for a significant portion of her life. Yes, she was a pastor at a few churches, but never left a church unless she was prompted by the Holy Spirit. She stayed at the church location for years on end, building up the community within and outside the congregation, and was actively involved in the lives of the people of this congregation. She was the shepherd of the flock.

Teacher

The role of the teacher is to educate and train individuals of the church. They carry wisdom and knowledge about the teachings of Jesus and share this with their students. Moses was a teacher and Jesus, among other names, was called teacher by people He ministered to.

*****

Take time to pray and ask the Holy Spirit what gifts you carry, if you don't already know, or maybe you have more to learn about. You are not limited to one gift, and you most likely will not receive them all at the same time. Be a good steward with what you have, and more will be given to you. Much like the story of the talents. You have been given talents and your master wants you to use and multiply them. When you do, He will give you more. Figure out what those are and act upon them. The world needs you! Refer to 1 Peter 4:10, "Each one should use whatever gift he [or she] has received to serve others."

The Bible gives us an analogy of the church as one body

composed of many parts. All these components are needed to form one body.[38] Though we as individuals represent different parts, we were all given the same Spirit that unites us. The Holy Spirit living inside of me is the same inside you. You were created for a purpose, though the premise of your purpose may change, and growth occurs within you as a person of faith, being a part of the body of Christ remains the same. It's up to you to contribute. Use what has been given to you and ask God how you can contribute to the body as a whole. This is an element of your purpose.

---

38   1 Corinthians 12:12-31

Chapter 11

Relationship with the Holy Spirit

One day while on the World Race in Cambodia, I sat in a small room where our luggage was stored. This was the only place I could find some solitude away from the kids running around, as well as from the other people in my group. I was drained. I was tired. I felt I had depleted my spirit. I had nothing left to give to others. This is when I learned the importance of self-care and how important quality time with Jesus is to pour out to others. I will never forget my time in that small space. I sat on top of the luggage, trying to get as comfortable as I could as sweat dripped off me from the humidity. God met me there. As I sat with headphones in my ears, I listened to the words of a song, and I felt as though God was singing the words to me.

The song is called *Come to Me* by Bethel Music. The words are spoken as though God is speaking to the listener. *I am the Lord your God. I go before you. I stand beside you.* Speaking of being *closer than your breath,* and being *all you need.*[39] It brought much comfort, as though I was sitting on God's lap as He sang these words to me. This song gave me reassurance of who God is and His location in my world. After cultivating a precious space where the Holy Spirit was present, I sat and listened and wrote down what I felt He was sharing with me. Words about my future, about my relationships, and about the journey I was currently on. He told me all about my future husband! A deep desire of mine. I didn't want this moment to end. It was incredible, one I will never forget. The Holy Spirit met me where I was because I created the time and the space to meet with Him. I began to learn the importance of our relationship and my role in it.

The more I walk with the Lord, the more I realize it is my responsibility to take ownership of my relationship with Him. To create the space to listen and be with Him; to invite Him into every part of my life. There is always more to be discovered about God. If we knew everything about Him we'd be overwhelmed. Our human brains would never be able to fathom the power and greatness of the God of this universe. It's a great mystery we will forever continue to unfold. How exciting is that?

God wants a relationship with us. Think of your loved ones. Do you make time to be with them? Do you laugh with them, cry with them? Do you go on adventures with them? Do you want to be around them? Think of God as a loved one. He wants to be with you, spend time with you, and join you on your adventures. The little stuff you care about, He cares about too. To keep a relationship alive, you must pour into the relationship from both sides. Am I right?

---

39 *Come to Me* by Jenn Johnson and Bethel Music

That's how it should be with God, Jesus, and the Holy Spirit. Spend time with Him. Strengthen your relationship. It doesn't come from you talking with someone else who then relays your message to God. That's not how it works. You have direct access to the God of the universe and He wants a relationship with you! Spend time with the one you desire to be like.

He will meet you where you are. He will meet you in the dark places. He will meet you in the sorrow. He will meet you in the pit. He will meet you in the storage closet. He will meet you there because He wants to pull you out. He wants you to reach out your hand, because He will grab it and pull you out of your dark places and into the light.

After this time in the small room, sitting on top of luggage and sweating, I felt more alive; I felt refreshed and renewed. My circumstances had not changed, but my heart, spirit, and mind had changed. It's all about perspective, your mindset, and spending time with the One who gives you life. This is what a relationship with the Creator looks like.

I want to emphasize the importance of this relationship, because it's not until you have a relationship with the Holy Spirit will you receive the gifts He wants to give you. You may experience Him in life, but it's not until you have a relationship with Him will you realize it has been Him the whole time. Once you realize it's Him, your day to day will change and you will start to experience miracles, visions, and dreams. You will become more aware of the miracles happening all around you. They are happening whether you acknowledge them or not.

A God You've Never Met: Who is the Holy Spirit?

Chapter 12

Visions and Dreams

*"In the last days," God says, "I will pour out my
Spirit on all people. Your sons and daughters will
prophesy,
Your young men will see visions,
Your old men will dream dreams.*

Acts 2:17

Visions

Rachel and I concluded our time in Costa Rica and met
up with our church group in Nicaragua. We were on the bus,
making our way back to home base for the week after a long
day of work. Everyone around me was either sleeping or
listening to music through their headphones. I was gazing out
the window watching the trees go by, when suddenly, as clear
as day, I saw myself on my wedding day. It was as though I
was a bystander looking up at myself at the altar. The Nikki
getting married was wearing a flowing white dress, a flower
crown, and the biggest smile. Standing in front of me was my

husband. We interlocked hands as I gazed into his eyes, but from my perspective I couldn't see his face. There was a glow, a bright light shining around us.

And then in an instant, this vision vanished, and the passing trees came back into view. I couldn't believe it! I looked around the bus and thought to myself, *Did anyone else just see that?* I was beside myself and could not stop smiling at what I had just seen. God had given me my first vision, a prophetic promise, and it's something I still hold close to my heart.[40]

God gives people visions and dreams to reveal His plan. In Genesis 15:1, the word of the Lord came to Abraham in a vision. The Lord showed Abraham the stars and told him as many as the number of stars would be the number of his offspring. That's a profound and direct vision. And even in this day and age, God continues to give dreams and visions to His people, which are His promises to us or a glimpse into how He wants to use us.

I was walking into church, the building was dark except for the stage lights beaming down on the worship band. The auditorium was filled with people standing, some with their hands raised. Everyone was frozen except for me, as I walked from the back of the auditorium down the aisle. As I walked, I noticed angels flying above everyone. Then I heard God say, "I am on the move, but not everyone can see it."

This was another vision. And I was not physically walking into church, I was sitting in my living room, surrounded by fellow believers praying for the church. We had been worshipping and asked the Holy Spirit to enter the room. Shortly after, He gave me this vision. This vision showed me

40 July 2012

how many people may be blinded to the ways of the Holy Spirit, but that does not mean He is not moving. God is at work in your life whether you see Him or not.

I was with my mom in Florida, visiting my Auntie Karen and cousin Kristin. We ventured over to Wakulla Springs, where we stayed for a few days, then made our way to Apalachicola, near the gulf. While we were in Apalachicola, a local suggested we check out St. George Island. Since we were on a spontaneous road trip, we decided to do it. To reach St. George Island, you must drive over a bridge. This island is a long, narrow strip, with one side on the gulf and the other on the bay.

Waterfront homes lined both sides. These houses were much different than the west coast houses I am used to, yet something seemed familiar. We drove to the end of the island, which is a state park, and dipped our toes in the sand. On the beach that day, I sensed I needed to see all the houses from the front, and I needed to go before sunset.

Auntie Karen, Kristin, and Mama agreed to go down the road toward the houses so I could get a better look. As Kristin drove, I looked out the window for a place with public beach access. Once we found access, I jumped out of the car and ran down the wooden path that led to the sandy beach.

When I approached the sand, I turned left to see the sun was setting behind me. As I walked, that familiarity increased. I felt as though I had been to this place before. No one else was around, my toes in the sand, the sun setting behind me, the houses facing the ocean, elevated on stilts, tall grass along the sand, swaying in the wind. It was something I had never seen before with my naked eye, and yet still so familiar. In this moment, walking along the beach, it hit me. Six months prior I had this exact vision.

This vision was of myself ten years older. I walked along the beach by myself as the sun set behind me. My toes in the sand, houses along the beach on stilts, tall grass swaying in the wind. I was out for a sunset walk, just me and Jesus. I walked up to a house with a white staircase leading from the sand to a back door. I climbed the stairs, and as I opened the door, I saw two kids running around the house while a man sat on a barstool at the counter. As I entered the doorway, this man turned to face me; his face lit up as he rose and walked toward me. He gave me a hug and kissed the top of my head, and in that moment, I knew this man was my husband.

Flash forward six months to St. George Island, and as I walked along the beach, I realized I was in that vision! I continued walking and scanned the houses, thinking, *could that same house be here?* I approached a white house with a white staircase leading up to a back door. I stood directly in front of this house and began to cry, overwhelmed by the sense that the Holy Spirit was with me. I felt as though I was in my vision, but ten years early. As I stood there with tears in my eyes, I heard God say, "This is what intimacy with Me looks like." It was an incredible breakthrough moment for me and I wanted more of this sweet, intimate relationship with Him.

I believe the Holy Spirit gives us visions to give us hope and keep us on track with where God wants to take us. I have had visions of owning a beach house, having a family of my own, speaking on stage, all which are deep desires of mine. These visions give me motivation, determination, and resilience to keep moving forward and to listen to the voice of God and the prompting of the Holy Spirit for which step to take next. God wants us to live a life of abundance, but we must do our part. It comes with obedience, hard work, and following the lead of the Holy Spirit.

The following visions are the catalyst for my desire to share the Holy Spirit in the church.

I found myself running up and down the aisles of my childhood church, laughing and waving my hands in the air. Everyone seated looked at one another, not knowing what to do. As I ran up and down the aisles, I called out, "The Holy Spirit is alive, and I am filled with Him."[41] In that vision I had a strong desire to share about the Holy Spirit with this church.

That same year, I had another vision. This time I was sitting in the balcony of another church. My mom was to the right of me, and a man I didn't know was on my left. To the right of my mom sat another man I didn't know. During worship, one of the worship leaders on the stage began jumping up and down. A huge smile covered her face as her head tilted toward heaven. I could sense the man next to me was a little uncomfortable, so I looked over at him and said, "Don't worry. It's the Holy Spirit."

It was the same with the man sitting next to my mom; he looked a little unsure so I told him it was the workings of the Holy Spirit. This explanation was all they needed to relax and enjoy the presence of our living God.

After I had reassured these men, a woman walked into the service. She was loud and disruptive, trying to interrupt the worship. I immediately sensed a darkness and knew she was not carrying the light of the Holy Spirit. She was on the main level of the auditorium, and somehow, I flew from the balcony to where she was. I immediately began praying and rebuking the evil spirit within her. She fell to the ground and was silenced. Meanwhile, the worship continued, growing

---

41 Year 2013

even louder throughout this experience. The lady left, and we continued in worship. The Holy Spirit was on the move.

You can experience visions too. They will come with pursuing a relationship with God. My very first vision appeared after a month of dedicated pursuit of Jesus. I was reading my Bible every day, identifying who God was to me, having open conversations with a trusted friend about God, and had a burning desire to know more. I prayed frequently for God to speak to me and give me dreams and visions. A month later He answered those prayers with a vision addressing a deep desire of mine.

Your timeline will most likely be different than mine. It may be a couple weeks, a few months, maybe even a year of pursuit before you receive a vision, but I don't want you to be discouraged. God sees you, He hears you, and He loves you. He wants to show you His plan for your life, but He wants to know He can trust you with this information, and building trust takes time. Keep praying, keep seeking, and it will happen. Specifically pray for a vision!

Dreams

The dreams and visions given to us by the Holy Spirit may occur months, even years, before they are fulfilled. Don't lose hope! Many of my visions have not been fulfilled, but they are the hope I hold onto that one day they will.

Mama and I were in the mountains for a girls' ski/snowboard trip. On the second night, I had a dream so vivid, when I woke up, I felt as though it really happened.

I was somewhere I didn't recognize, but having fun I know for sure. I saw my grandma standing in front of me.[42] She was smiling, healthy, and the way I remembered her as the fun,

42 Year of dream 2013

energetic grandma she once was. She glowed. I stood in shock as Grandma, who was not alive anymore on this earth, stood in front of me. She said to me in a calm, sweet voice, "I was sent here from God to give you reassurance and hope."

My eyes wide, I asked her, "For what?" I was so confused as to what was going on, but she just smiled and looked at me with a peaceful, deep love.

It was a precious moment I didn't want to end. In my dream, tears filled my eyes because I knew she would be leaving me. I woke up with those tears still in my eyes; I felt as though I'd just been with Grandma!

Many questions ran through my mind when I awoke, but one thing was for sure. God sent my grandma—whom I miss so much—to visit me! It was a bright, vibrant dream. I later learned dreams of bright color are from God.

Joseph was a young man of seventeen who tended his flock with his brothers. He had dreams of his brothers bowing down to him. When he told his brothers of the dreams, they plotted to kill him because they were jealous. Instead they sold him into slavery.

In the midst of his despair, God remained with Joseph. Thirteen years later, Joseph became Pharaoh's right-hand man, in charge of all of Egypt after using his gift of the Spirit to interpret a dream of Pharaoh's no one else could.[43] When Pharaoh asked Joseph to interpret his dream, Joseph gave God the credit by responding "I cannot do it, but God will give Pharaoh the answer he desires."[44] Pharaoh later asked, "Can we find anyone like this man, one in whom is in the spirit of God?"[45]

43 Genesis 41

44 Genesis 41:16

45 Genesis 41:38

During a time of famine, Joseph took pity on his family who had sold him into slavery and gave them food. When he did so, they bowed down to him. Joseph's dream had come true! God had given Joseph those dreams thirteen years prior to prepare him for what was to come.[46]

I asked my friend Gary, who was my coach along with his wife while on the World Race, for some answers about dream interpretation. He has this gift and has gone through a Master Certification process to further his knowledge, so I knew he could give me some insight. Here are some questions I asked him.

How do we know a dream is from God?

Gary replied that most dreams from God are bright and colorful. Nonetheless, not all dreams from God are that way. Dreams are usually "revelatory and/or redemptive," which means addressing your calling, healing, prophetic, or encouraging. Gary said there are different categories of dreams; for example, dreams from the enemy or regarding the soul, such as our own heart's imagination, or warning dreams from God. Dark dreams or those in black and white are most likely not from God. Granted, He can use any dream to bring a message to the dreamer.

How does one interpret a dream?

Gary's direct response was, "Dream interpretation requires being able to hear from Holy Spirit. Of course, to be a dream interpreter, there needs to be a level of gifting, training, and development of the gift, but the Holy Spirit is

46 Genesis 37

vital to understanding dreams. Asking the Holy Spirit and sitting quietly in His presence can open your heart to hear. But it is always good to get the wisdom or insight of others as well and no big decisions should be made based on one dream alone." Gary gave further advice when I interviewed him for my podcast. He said to value the dream, focus on the dream, write it down, have intimacy with God, and through the Holy Spirit He will help you interpret. He also mentioned, "The hardest dreams to interpret are your own dreams because you are too close to them." However, when interpreting dreams the most important thing you can do is go to God and ask Him what He is communicating with you.

Why do some people dream more than others?

Gary answered that some people just have more dreams than others. There are times when a person may dream a lot, and times when dreams are few. Prophetic people tend to have more dreams, but not always. Some have more because they ask! Some have more because they place higher value on their dreams than other people, and if you are faithful in the little, God will give you much. Some people write their dreams down as they remember them, adding value, even if only a small bit. Gary gave some great introductory insight on dream interpretation. I am thankful for him and the knowledge he is willing to share. I know this was helpful to me, and I hope it is for you.

Mark Batterson states, "God-given dreams won't contradict scripture." He also says, "The meaning of dreams isn't always immediately discernible. If Peter had to process dreams, we probably will too. Some dreams make immediate sense, but others won't make sense for decades.

And dreams are like doors; often one leads to another, which leads to another."[47]

I believe God gives visions and dreams as a glimpse of what is to come, or guidance for what He wants us to do, and to keep our hope rooted in Him. God gives us promises and He keeps those promises; however, they most likely will not happen on our own timeline. Release the timeline you have for your life and hold onto the promises God has given you. Pray specifically for God-given dreams!

Visit From Heaven

Once, during a corporate worship service, I felt as if heaven and earth were colliding. It was as if things of heaven were coming down to earth and all the saints and angels were in one room together. The presence of the Holy Spirit was so overwhelming in the room that I was flat on my face, lying on my stomach on the floor.

As I lie on the floor, worshipping, I felt the presence of someone else worshipping with me. Yes, there were many other people physically in the room, but I felt as if someone were with me spiritually, someone I dearly love who went home to be with Jesus six years prior. That presence was my dear grandma! What a beautiful moment. I felt as though Grandma and I were worshipping our God together! Tears of joy streamed down my face. She and I were laughing together and singing praises to our Savior.

When Grandma was alive, she told of a similar experience she had with her friend Ruby. After Ruby passed, Grandma would have feelings as though Ruby were with her. She acknowledged the feeling by saying, "Ruby, I miss you." And then the feeling was gone. I believe in those precious

---

47 *Whisper: How to Hear the Voice of God* by Mark Batterson

moments, God sent Ruby to visit Grandma just as God sent Grandma to visit me. And I also believe just as God sends loved ones, He sends angels.

A God You've Never Met: Who is the Holy Spirit?

Chapter 13

I See Angels

Do not forget to entertain strangers for by so doing some people have entertained angels without knowing it.

Hebrews 13:2

Grandma would often say, "Treat everyone with love and respect because you never know when you are entertaining angels." It wasn't until years later did I realize these words come from the Bible. Grandma knew the Bible like the back of her hand, and I did not appreciate her knowledge until I grew older.

I did not understand this statement when I was younger. I had heard about angels, but didn't fully believe they were real and among us. This was a concept my mind could not comprehend. I was too much in my head, trying to think logically. I couldn't see them, so how could they be real? This is where faith comes in.

I have heard stories of people being visited by who they

thought were angels. The more I learned about the Holy Spirit, the more curious I became and wanted to know for myself.

Grandma had told me a story she claimed taught her about faith and the Lord's provision. One day, during the Great Depression, there was no bread for lunches when she and her siblings left for school. Their mother instructed them to come home for lunch, which she recalls was not a short walk. When they arrived at home, their mother still did not have anything for them to eat. At that very moment, there was a knock on the door and a man stood before them with a loaf of bread to advertise a new bakery in the area. Their mother walked back in the house with her eyes full of hope, lifted up the loaf of bread, and exclaimed, "The Lord will provide."

Grandma told me this story many times growing up, and when she did, she would say the man at the door was an angel. When she and her family looked for the baker later to thank him, there was no such bakery in town! Grandma believed, as well as I, the Lord sent him to provide food for her family.

When I was visiting my dear friend Erica in Colorado, she shared with me a story about a friend of hers (we will call him Tyler) and his experience of entertaining an angel. Tyler's mom passed away, but during her fight with cancer, Erica prayed, and God gave her a picture of a swing to draw, not knowing the importance of what it meant. Later, Erica learned swings were Tyler's mother's happy place, the place she enjoyed and loved escaping to. Erica told me there is a painting that hangs in Tyler's office of a little girl on a swing. And when Erica asked Tyler how he got the painting, he told her this story.

One day, Tyler went to a church service and on the stage was a painting of a little girl on a swing. He knew he had to have this painting because it reminded him of his mom. After the service, he asked the staff who had painted this picture because he wanted to buy it. No one knew where it had come from. Frantically, he wandered around the church, asking whomever he saw if they knew who had painted this piece. Tyler then saw an older man approach the stage to gather the painting. He ran to him and told him he must have this painting and would pay anything for it. The older man smiled, nodded, handed Tyler the painting, and turned and walked away. Tyler asked the staff about this older man, but no one knew who he was. And no one else had seen him. This is when Tyler realized the older man must have been an angel.

I read the book *The Veil* by Blake Healy, and in it he shares his experiences of seeing angels and demons from a young age. He writes about being able to see in the spiritual realm.

Reading the words in this book deepened my desire to see for myself. I wanted to see angels. I wanted to be able to see in the spiritual realm.

I prayed for God to show me angels. I asked Him to be able to see in the spiritual realm. I prayed these prayers for months. I would practice closing my eyes and looking in my mind's eye. DC Talk has a song titled *Mind's Eye*. If you don't know who DC Talk is, they are a '90s Christian band I grew up listening to. I loved their music. I would sing along and make up interpretive dance moves with my sister. Anyway, in *Mind's Eye*, they describe God as unseen as the wind, and seeing Him in your mind's eye. In the song, DC Talk uses a clip of Billy Graham preaching, "Can you see God? Have you ever seen him? I've never seen the wind. I've seen effects of the wind, but I've never seen the wind. There's a mystery to it." This is how I view the Holy Spirit and seeing angels.

In due time, God answered my prayer.

Three months before leaving for the World Race, those I

participated with and I went to training camp to help prepare us for our upcoming eleven-month adventure. At training camp we experienced spiritual warfare. The devil tried what he could to rip our group apart by using a member of our group to go a little crazy and run away from camp. When you say yes to God, Satan will do what he can to deter you from doing what God has called you to do. If he tries to do this in your life, that's when you know something big is about to happen in a God way. We battled and prayed all night, but in the midst of chaos that's when it happened.

During our training week, my squad and I lived in tents in the middle of a field in Tennessee. A few other girls and I decided it would be a good idea to pray over the tent of the guy from our group who was under spiritual attack, as well as pray protection over all of us. So at 1:00 am, we stood around his tent, which he was not in, stretched out our hands and began to pray.

I closed my eyes and began praying for deliverance for this guy and for protection over all of us. Suddenly, I saw three angels appear. They were ten feet tall and wearing all white, with long, flowing hair that reached to their mid-backs, and held staffs even taller than them in their hands. The angels were strategically placed all around our tents. They looked strong and determined. I wasn't scared. I felt a sense of peace, safety, and protection. God was showing me He had sent His angels to protect us. I laughed in awe and told the other girls what I saw. One of them responded, "I see them too."

It was a spectacular experience that cannot be explained logically. It happened because of faith, because I believed God would show up in that moment. I slept so well that night!

Seeing angels is not something that happens to me regularly. However, I feel God shows them to me in my mind's eye in specific situations. I can sense when they are around me. During this particular moment, my eyes were closed, and it was as though I were given a vision of them surrounding us. You might or might not see angels when your eyes are open. There have been times when I look up with my eyes open and sense angels in the corners near the ceiling of the room I'm in, especially when singing praises to God. They are worshipping Him with us!

Angels are called "ministers of the wind and fire." When the day of Pentecost came, wind and fire entered the upper room where the disciples were waiting for the Holy Spirit. The Holy Spirit was ushered in by angels. In Psalm 104, God rides upon the wind. Angels usher God into a place. God uses angels as messengers. He could deliver His messages Himself, but He uses His creation according to their design. God used Gabriel to tell Mary she would give birth to the Son of God. God used a man who owned a bakery to give my grandma and her family bread, an old man to give Tyler a painting, and He sent His angels to show me we were safe in our tents.

These are just some of the many stories I know of people interacting with angels. Do you have a story yourself? Or is it time for you to have your own story?

A God You've Never Met: Who is the Holy Spirit?

Chapter 14

Do You Believe in Miracles?

I will show wonders in the heaven above
And signs in the earth below.

Acts 2:19

Do you believe in miracles? Do you believe the miracles in the Bible still happen today?

These are two questions I asked a church group I had the opportunity to speak in front of while on a mission trip in Belize. Less than half raised their hands. At one point in my life I was like them, and maybe you are too. I would read the stories in the Bible, but not believe they still happened today. How could they? I was stuck inside my head, overanalyzing, and trying to think logically, when I wanted to believe it was true so badly in my heart.

During month two of the World Race, God rocked my world and shifted my belief. Before then I was in disbelief and questioning God and His supernatural powers. But He proved Himself to be a God of miracles through the act of the Holy Spirit.

I was in Tegucigalpa, Honduras, walking down the dirt streets of a very poor community. We walked house to house, praying for people and offering them an opportunity to be a part of a food program. Toward the end of the long day, my six teammates and I made our way to the bus. One of my teammates, Christina, walked significantly slower than the rest of us. I stopped and waited for her to catch up and asked if she was okay. She said her back hurt so bad she could barely walk and had numbness down her leg.

In that very moment I felt the need to pray for her, but I told her we would wait until we got to the bus. God literally stopped me in my tracks and convicted me to pray in the moment. As I stood, I turned toward her to say, "No! I am going to pray for you now!" She agreed, and as we slowly made our way to the bus, I placed my hand on her back and prayed for healing. I prayed for buckets of healing to be poured down from heaven. I declared God did not want His children to be in pain but to dance with Him. God is the ultimate physician who could and would heal her! I praised Him for what He was about to do—heal my friend!

When I finished praying, I looked at her and asked, "How do you feel?" She was silent, her mouth and eyes wide open.

"Nikki," she paused.

"I don't feel any pain."

I chuckled, "Are you kidding me?"

"Nikki, I wouldn't lie to you. The pain is gone!"

We were both stunned and speechless. Christina and I looked as though we had just seen a ghost. She and I turned slowly in a bit of shock and headed for the bus. We sat silently next to each other. She put her legs up on the seat in front of her and looked at me wide-eyed, "I couldn't sit like this before."

I was shocked. God used me to heal my friend's back. That night I couldn't sleep, still in awe of God and the Holy Spirit and His power. I sat on a blanket in the middle of a grass field under the stars and talked with God. During this time, God shared with me how my brother would be healed from epilepsy and my dad would be a believer. I cried and thanked God for sharing this with me. What a big day! My belief in miracles changed that day; I realized the miracles from the Bible still happen today!

We have the Spirit within us, but He comes upon us when others are involved. In this moment with Christina, the Holy Spirit came upon me to heal her. The same power that rose Jesus from the grave is inside me and inside of you! Do you believe it?

Two months later, in Costa Rica, we walked from house to house praying for the people who lived there. This is something I noticed is more acceptable in third world countries, which is why we did it often. Most of the people were very welcoming and invited us into their homes.

We were welcomed into a home where the mother of the household complained of back pain. She was hunched over and shuffling her feet. She had been praying for a doctor to come because she could not afford to go to a clinic. The group called me out and motioned for me to pray healing over this lady. The word got out that God used me to heal Christina's back, so why not this woman too?

I walked over to her and placed my hand on the very spot she felt pain. There were about fourteen others surrounding us, praying in agreement. I prayed for buckets of healing to be poured down on her and for her pain to be released. I prayed for God as the ultimate physician to heal her. When I finished praying, I asked this woman how she was feeling. She began to cry and rejoice. She exclaimed, "My pain is gone! My pain is gone!" She wiggled, danced, lifted her hands in the air, and explained how she hadn't been able to do that in a long time. She was overwhelmed and overcome with joy because she had been praying for a doctor, and the ultimate physician showed up at her doorstep. It was not me. It was the Holy Spirit, but He used my willing heart to be His vessel and touch His hurting child. I couldn't believe God used me a second time. It was a very humbling experience. Even now I think back and the experience renews my faith.

The Holy Spirit wants to partner with us to perform miracles. Take the story in the Bible of Jesus feeding the 5,000. Jesus asked for whatever the people had to give, and a young boy stepped up and gave Jesus his small lunch. Jesus blessed and multiplied the food. Imagine if the young boy didn't offer Jesus his lunch, didn't step up and give what he had. Do you think the 5,000 would have been fed? Do you think a miracle would have happened?[48]

The Holy Spirit waited for me to volunteer to pray and lay hands on Christina in the middle of the street, and Jesus waited until the boy offered his lunch. He wants to partner with us to show His glory and deepen our faith. God can heal and feed people all on his own, but He chooses to use us. He includes us in His story for the lives of others. We need to pray for miracles to happen in each other's lives more often.

He performs wonders that cannot be fathomed,
miracles that cannot be counted.

Job 9:10

---

48 John 6

While I was in Swaziland, I lived at an orphanage with my forty-two fellow squad mates. Because of my athletic training and sports medicine background, I was asked to run the medical clinic. Only in a third world country! I agreed, not having a clue what to expect. Along with me was my squad mate Jessica, who had just graduated from nursing school; Zach, with plans to apply to medical school; and Amanda, with plans to pursue nursing when she returned home. We lacked experience, but that didn't stop us! We were excited for the opportunity.

We were told people from the surrounding villages would come for treatment. And they did. Some people walked many miles to see us. They would arrive exhausted and thirsty from the journey. Even though the clinic got a little hectic at times, we were able to provide some services needed, and most importantly, we were able to pray with each patient who walked through the doors.

One lady came through the door and immediately sat down on a bench. She looked tired and in pain. I asked her what was going on, and she described a migraine she was experiencing. Yes, we could give her medication, but in that moment, we decided to pray for her and asked the Holy Spirit to come. I laid hands on her head and declared for the pain to be gone in Jesus' name. After the first prayer she looked up and said the pain was starting to go away. That wasn't good enough. We prayed again for God to heal her. She looked up and said the pain was a little better, but still there. We prayed a third time, buckets of healing to be poured upon her from heaven and for God to release the pain in her head. She looked up with a smile of relief on her face and said, "It's gone." Praise Jesus!

I don't know why it took three times praying for God to heal her, but I know with each prayer, faith increased. We were taking steps closer to the Father with each prayer and ushering into His presence.

You may be reading these stories and thinking, "Nah, those stories aren't real." For one, I would never lie to you. And two, try it for yourself. I dare you. Test that doubt of yours, and believe me, God will blow your doubt out of the water. I don't want you to just take my word for it. I don't want you to hear my stories or the stories of my friends; I want you to experience them yourself. Ask God to show up and He will. Ask God for a miracle and He will do it. All He wants you to do is ask Him (Matthew 7:7-8).

Miracle Through Forgiveness

Grandma received a call from the Christian Broadcasting Network (CBN), asking if she could go to her local hospital to pray for a woman who was dying of cancer. This woman's aunt, who lived in the Midwest, had sent a request to CBN for a minister to go and pray for her relative. When Grandma arrived, she found the woman in a coma, lying in her hospital bed. Her husband sat beside her and said to my grandma, "I did this to her." He confessed to Grandma that he was filled with anger toward his father, who had since passed away. Evidently, this man's father mistreated his mother. He showed his hands to Grandma and said, "See these hands? I hate these hands, because they are my father's hands. I have wanted to cut them off, so great was my hatred."

Grandma told this story to a psychologist friend of hers and asked if a person could become ill through someone else's anger. And yes, it's true. As the couple had been together, his anger exploded and he externalized it, while she internalized it.

This man was in a position to forgive his father and repent. Grandma prayed with him as he asked God for forgiveness. Shortly after this encounter, Grandma decided she should leave for the day. On her next visit, the woman had been moved to the ICU because the cancer spread throughout her body. Many people were interceding and praying on her behalf, even Grandma's congregation.

The next time Grandma went to the hospital, she was surprised to find the woman sitting up in bed, smiling. God was at work. Her family and children surrounded her smiling and praising God.

Because this man was able to let go and forgive, God released healing and a miracle occurred. Don't let your bitterness and anger get in the way of a miracle in your life or that of a loved one. This is exactly what Satan wants you to do. And believe me, he is real.

A God You've Never Met: Who is the Holy Spirit?

Chapter 15

The Devil is Real

The Lord said to Satan, "Where have you come from?" Satan answered the Lord, "From roaming throughout the earth, going back and forth on it."

Job 1:7

In Nicaragua during the World Race, I, along with my team, lived in a house called the Castle, because it looked like one. This was a place of refuge for women to come during the day who were caught in prostitution. They were told about the God who loves them and how to be set free.

One day, a few of my teammates and I were in the house with the women. A teenage girl was among them, along with her mom and sister. All three of them were captive in prostitution, which is a dark and evil life. During worship, I felt the presence of the Holy Spirit. However, there was another presence that was not of God. I raised my hands in prayer to be filled with the Holy Spirit. Tears filled my eyes and a smile covered my face because I knew the Holy Spirit was filling me for what was to come.

During worship, this teenage girl began shaking, but this did not feel like the Holy Spirit. It wasn't a peaceful or joyous shaking, like some experience with the Holy Spirit. A few leaders directed her to the couch to lie down. I walked over to the couch to find her angry, and the leaders hovered over her, praying. Something felt different, and I realized these women were praying with authority for Satan to leave. All of a sudden, this girl began to scream and thrash about. She screamed as though she were in a horror movie. Her eyes rolled back; she kicked and tried to pull out her hair. Two of the leaders grabbed her arms to hold them down and I jumped in and grabbed hold of her legs. As we held her down to protect herself and others, a voice from her mouth spoke, "She's mine. You are all whores."

We immediately started praying fiercely against Satan and praying for Jesus to come. Every time we would say the name of Jesus she would scream, "Noooo!" and tell us to shut up. We read scripture over her, and she would scream more. Her eyes were dark and would roll back into her head. Something had taken over her body. We prayed, declared Jesus over her, and held her down for two hours!

During those long hours, I became frustrated because it was taking so long, but I wasn't going to stop fighting for her life. I cried as my heart broke for her. At one point, her mom came over, knelt down beside her, and began sobbing and saying this was all her fault. One of the leaders knelt down beside her, wrapping her arms around her, and told her this wasn't her fault and that Jesus could save her and her daughter. Through her sobs, the mother said she wanted to be saved by Jesus!

After two hours of intense prayer and reading truth from scripture over this girl, she grew calmer and closed her eyes. Tension stretched across her forehead and her eyes moved back and forth under her eyelids. She did not look peaceful. We continued praying.

She opened her eyes, and we noticed they were not black like they once were. She looked up at me and I smiled at her. She immediately looked away. I continued smiling at her, and when she looked at me again, she faintly smiled back. I was slightly concerned because I didn't have complete peace, and she still seemed a little tense. Maybe she was overwhelmed by the number of people surrounding her when she came back to it, or she was exhausted, I don't know. When asked if she believed Jesus loves her, she nodded. She no longer screamed when we would say the name of Jesus. We sat her up and let her rest. I have to believe, and trust God is with her and continuing to speak truth to her, because once she walked out the front door, I never saw her again.

I believe Satan and demons exist. The Bible says they do, but to experience something like what happened in Nicaragua first hand makes it even more real. This was one of the craziest things I have ever seen. Satan comes in all forms. He comes like he did with this vulnerable girl, or through the feeling of heaviness or tension in your body. Or in the form of lies poured into your mind about yourself. There is a spiritual battle going on and we must be aware. What we experienced in the end was the power of Jesus. There is power in the name of Jesus. In moments during those two hours when I didn't know what to pray, I repeated over and over, "Jesus, Jesus, Jesus..."

It may have taken two exhausting hours, but the Holy Spirit was with us. He was in battle with us, fighting for this teenage girl. Evil is present in this world, which we cannot defeat on our own; victory happens only by the power of God, by the power of the Holy Spirit, and the power of two or more gathering together in the name of Jesus. Spiritual warfare is happening, and we need to acknowledge that the devil is real and "prowling around like a roaring lion looking for someone to devour."[49] Nonetheless, be confident in the authority we have in Jesus and the victory that is already ours because of the blood of Jesus. He sacrificed Himself in order for us to be victorious over evil. We have been given tools to defeat Satan, but we cannot do it without the power of the Holy Spirit. It's not about preparing for if he comes, but when.

> *For our struggle is not against flesh and blood,*
> *but against the rulers, against the authorities,*
> *against the powers of this dark world and against*
> *the spiritual forces of evil in the heavenly realms.*

Ephesians 6:12

We cannot underestimate Satan, but he is not original. I have experienced what it was like going into battle without the armor of God. A couple of my friends were working through some heavy things and I wanted to be there for them. I wanted to offer my support and fight with them through their struggle. I didn't want to take on the burden, but to be a sounding board and someone to offer advice from an outside perspective and pray with them. This is exactly what I was doing. After two days of fighting, I felt off. I felt a heaviness upon me and I was on the verge of tears in an overwhelming, about-to-break kind of way. I didn't know what was going on with me. A few days

---

49 1 Peter 5:8

later, I felt as though I had been hit by a truck! I was exhausted! I was fighting a battle unprepared. I came to realize I walked into this battle without armor on, without protection for myself. I was praying for protection for my friends, but not for me. And as I prayed for my friends, I had no one praying for me. I stepped onto the battlefield and was exposed to Satan's flaming arrows. This is like going snowboarding without any of the proper gear—snow jacket and pants, goggles, gloves, helmet, board, and boots. I would never go on the mountain without any of these items, which is how I need to view each day as I battle against Satan. I learned a valuable lesson that day, never start a day without putting on the armor of God because you never know what your day will bring, and you must always be prepared.

When I saw angels, it was within spiritual warfare, but Jesus won, and He proved His own presence by sending angels and revealing them to us. He died on the cross and conquered death, so we could be victorious and set free.

You must believe in the victory for your own life. Satan will do whatever he can to tear you down, and you cannot give in to him. If you don't know what to do in pain and warfare, say the name of Jesus over and over. This will set your mind on the things above and redirect your focus to the only One who can defeat evil.

I saw Satan fall like lightning from heaven. I have given you authority to trample on snakes and scorpions and to overcome all the power of the enemy; nothing will harm you.

Luke 10:18-19

*****

I was on vacation in Italy with my family. We rented a villa in Lake Como to celebrate my dad's sixtieth birthday. Italy is a beautiful place. All the food is fresh, the people are not in a rush, (except on the road— now I know where my dad gets it! It's deep in his Italian roots), and they know the importance of family and community and spending time together.

We flew into Milan and my parents rented a car to drive to Lake Como. Late in the night, we arrived after hours at the villa office to pick up our key, which was left in a lock box for us. It took a bit of time to find our villa because the navigation and streets are not clearly marked. We eventually found it, and by this time it was about 10 pm.

We tried to unlock the gate, but the key didn't work. We were tired from traveling all day, in a foreign country no less, and just wanted to go to bed. We called the agency and learned someone had left the wrong key for us. Dad went back to the office to pick up the correct key as the rest of us waited for him by the locked gate.

We finally make our way inside the gate to find a beautiful courtyard with a fountain in the middle and a pathway we followed leading up to our front door. As we opened the door and made our way inside, we noticed strange pictures throughout the house. In the entryway hung a five-foot picture of a naked woman jumping rope. Paintings of colonial people with eyes that seem to follow you throughout the house. In my room hung two paintings, side by side. One was a peaceful scene of a little girl in white with a glow around her head. An angel hovered over her. The other painting showed another little girl, but this painting was dark, with a demon peering over the little girl's shoulder. It was so creepy, I took it off the wall immediately.

A narrow spiral staircase led up to a loft. I started up the stairs, and as soon as I approached the top I felt as though I had been hit with a ton of bricks on my chest. A heaviness and a darkness surrounded this space much more than in the rest of the house. I had a feeling we were not alone. Oddly enough, my mom, my brother Chris, and his girlfriend Megan felt the same. I decided to take a shower before heading to bed, but the entire time I felt as though someone was watching me. I kept looking over my shoulder to see who was there. I couldn't see anyone, but something was there.

That same night, Chris went up to the loft and looked in the mirror. He noticed a figure standing behind him, and at the same time his nose began to bleed. It freaked him out! That was it. I gathered Mom, Chris, and Megan and told them we needed to pray and take authority over this space in the name of Jesus. And we needed to start in the loft. The four of us climbed the spiral staircase and I began declaring the name of Jesus and inviting the Holy Spirit to come. I spoke Jesus' name into every corner, nook, and cranny. I prayed with authority and told Satan to leave and to take his demons with him. My mom prayed in agreement and then prayed for the family who owned the house. Deep in my spirit I knew this is exactly who we needed to pray for and I exclaimed, "Yes!" followed by a laughing spell because this happens often when I am in the presence of the Holy Spirit.

I walked the perimeter of the loft while praying and waving my hands over everything. I wanted to push out the darkness and I know the Holy Spirit was doing so. Sometimes we need to physically act out what we want to occur. This creates an energy and puts us in the act of doing something about the situation. It's also another way to usher in the Holy Spirit, like fanning a flame and creating wind. The Holy Spirit is the fire and the wind, and we partner with Him against

Satan. We prayed for peace, and moments after praying, I felt a peace which transcends all understanding.[50]

I still didn't want to stay in this villa, even after we prayed. The next day we went to the agency to switch houses. Although I was optimistic we'd be able to move, not a single villa was available. There was nothing we could do. We had to stay where we were.

Every night I fell asleep listening to worship music. During the day I would walk around the house regularly declaring it as Jesus' space. My sister joined us a few days into our trip and the loft became her room. On her first night, she sensed someone in the room with her. From then on, she and I would sit on her bed every night and pray for the protection of Jesus and for the presence of the Holy Spirit to be with her.

Even though this was an unusual experience, I know God brought us there for a reason. My mom later told me when she looked into booking a villa, this was the only one available for the exact days we needed. God set us up. I believe He wanted us there to bring His light into the darkness. At first, I was upset about staying there, but the more I thought about it, the more I realized there was a reason. This experience also brought my family closer. Praying like that together will unite you, and those times sitting on my sister's bed were precious moments of being with her and sharing Jesus together. Moments I will never forget.

The day we left, we wrote a note to the family who owned the house. We told them how we prayed for them and prayed for peace and light among them. We blessed them with love and hope that they would feel the presence of God in their home. To this day we have no idea if they received the note, but I hope they sensed a difference as soon as they walked in.

50 Philippians 4:7

We may never know, but I do know God is there and I know He used us. Seeds have been planted and we may never see the fruit of those seeds. And that's ok.

Demons are real, but God has given us the authority to overcome. Pray like you mean it. Wave your hands if you need to. You will not be defeated when God is on your side. "For everyone born of God overcomes the world. This is the victory that has overcome the world, even our faith. Who is it that overcomes the world? Only the one who believes that Jesus is the Son of God." (1 John 5:4-5)

*****

Grandma shared a story about demonic spirits and darkness she experienced before I was born with a friend of hers. After her passing, I found a copy of this story typed in a letter to her friend. This is a paraphrase of what she wrote.

A couple who had once been members of the church she pastored had turned against her for some unknown reason. The woman hosted a luncheon and invited some church women, excluding Grandma. One of Grandma's friends who attended later shared how she felt a demonic spirit the whole time, and while she was eating, she started choking and became nauseous. The hostess had been speaking against her former church and its leadership.

Six days after this luncheon, Caleb, my mom's dog who stayed at her parents' house, died in the middle of the night. He was a healthy, sweet dog who didn't have any health issues, so this was a shock. Grandpa found him in the morning, stretched out on the patio, dead.

The next evening at church, Grandma's friend came up to her and said, "I didn't sleep all night last night because I was praying for you. Around one o'clock something strange happened. I don't know if I should tell you or not." Grandma encouraged her to share.

Her friend continued, "It was death." Grandma told her about Caleb and began to question, "Was death directed toward me, and the prayers of God's people saved me?" Another friend was praying for her the same night.

An autopsy revealed Caleb died of severe shock. There was blood throughout his abdomen and intestines. The vet didn't know what had caused the shock.

Sometimes the enzymes in the pancreas are triggered and attack the pancreas, but this usually happens with a very old dog, mostly female, and after a fatty meal. None of this was true about Caleb.

God doesn't make these things happen. So why doesn't He stop it? There is evil in this world, and God gives us a choice to seek Him or to run from Him. He wants us to cling to Him and when we do, He will turn the bad into something good. This is the beauty in it. He is our hope in this dark and evil world. And He is our light and victory!

Grandma shared about the victory she felt after death passed over her home. Her life was spared. A price was paid, but in the end she was victorious.

There is a spiritual world around us in which angels walk with us and protect us; where demons try to destroy us; but where the Holy Spirit is alive, fighting with us and for us. There is nothing to fear when God is on our side. He is bigger than anything that comes our way.

Chapter 16

The Red Light District

In Phuket, Thailand, I walked the streets of the Red Light District with my team from the World Race. It was 10:30 at night as we made our way down Bangla Road in Patong Beach in observation. It was dark, and yet the street was lit up with neon lights. Music blared from every direction as visitors and tourists filled the streets and bars. Ladyboys dressed in exotic costumes and heels. Women stood on the side of the road, wearing heels and short dresses. Bar promoters held signs and menus motioning for people to come inside. I'd never seen anything like this before.

As I looked closer and became aware of my surroundings, I noticed people seeking pleasure, and I felt a sense of loneliness come over me. I also noticed the bar promoters' menus were for shows and purchasing women. When I remember this time, that same pit returns to my stomach. This was my first experience in any form of a Red Light District, and Patong Beach is one of the most popular in Phuket.

Back at home base, we gathered as a group of twenty to pray for the night ahead of us. The group was split in two. Half would go out into the Red Light District, and the other half would stay behind to pray and intercede. We were preparing for battle and would need back up. Some would be on the front lines in the chaos and others on the front lines in the spiritual battle. Walking those streets and entering those bars, knowing a group of people were praying for us and didn't stop until we returned was a comforting thought.

When we arrived at the District, we split up into smaller groups of three to four. We had to remain discreet as to why we were there. No one could know we were missionaries. My group decided to start by walking the street and praying, asking the Holy Spirit to point us in the direction He wanted us to go; to point out a specific person to talk to. I felt so uncomfortable and uneasy, yet my eyes were open to the darkness in this place. Older, foreign men walked among us with young girls linked under their arms—their purchases for the night. Women stood along the street, waiting for someone to approach them and pay for their services for the night. Ladyboys walked around in their exotic costumes, promoting their shows. Russian girls danced in cages up against windows to be seen by onlookers. All of these people had something in common, they were slaves to the darkness.

People filled the first establishment we walked into. Barely- dressed women pole danced on tables, trying to look sexy and attract attention. Looking closely, I could see how miserable they were. They did not want to be there, but they were caught in this life because they thought it was a way to provide for their family, or they were trafficked, and now they couldn't leave.

I sat on a bar stool. I noticed how the girl behind the counter looked so young. She asked me if I wanted a drink and I politely declined and asked what her name was. In her broken English, she told me a name that I knew was not her own (this was common). I asked her how old she was, and she answered that she was fourteen. My heart broke. I asked her how she got the job. She told me her aunt owns the bar and she had just started working that month. She was looking forward to making money. I noticed a Connect Four game next to me. I smiled at the young bartender and asked if she wanted to play with me. So in the middle of the chaos surrounding us, she and I played Connect Four. We laughed together and enjoyed ourselves in those short moments.

Our mission as a group was to give these girls at least twenty minutes of freedom and a breath of fresh air, and tell them how valuable and loved they are. We met them where they were and did not force anything on them. We asked questions about them specifically, and in those conversations they'd usually ask, "Who are you? You are different. Why are you here in a place like this?" This was the open door to share about Jesus and give them a sense of hope. It was in those moments the light shown in the darkness. Some of them wanted to know more, and with those girls we would arrange to grab coffee or lunch the next day.

Everything in me wanted to rescue every girl I laid eyes on. We weren't even allowed to talk to the Russian girls because they were under strict surveillance and could only be approached by men who were there to pay for them. It makes me angry to think of these girls who are trapped, and brings tears to my eyes as I recall the faces I saw that night. These young girls were miserable, in pain, disrespected, and manipulated. This was a sight I will never forget.

After we returned to home base late into the night, all twenty of us would gather together and debrief on the events of the night. The intercessors would share words and feelings and visions the Holy Spirit had revealed to them. Those of us out in the bars would share how God showed up in the darkness. It was a beautiful thing, and many times we discovered overlap among our experiences. We knew the Holy Spirit was present and on the move!

This experience is one I will never forget. And it was not the only time I walked the streets of the Red Light District.

Wipe Every Tear is a ministry that rescues girls throughout Southeast Asia, and I had the opportunity to partner with them in the Philippines. This ministry offers a safe house, food, education, and discipleship for women trapped in the sex trade industry. I, along with my parents, had the opportunity to work with this amazing ministry.

The first week of month nine on the World Race was "Parent Vision Trip" (PVT). Parents have the opportunity to join their son or daughter on the mission field and participate in ministry. I had the privilege of having both of my parents join me. This was an answered prayer and a work of the Holy Spirit from the start. Because my dad is not a believer, he was not set on the idea when I talked with my parents about the opportunity. My mom, however, was all in, but felt she was not supposed to go without Dad. I agreed. I prayed and asked God what to do about this situation. He told me to fast. At this point in my faith journey I had never done a fast for a specific request before. But I knew something had to be done.

I shared what God wanted me to do with my dear friends and teammates, Erica and David, and together we decided to fast and pray for our families for the next twenty-four hours.

The end of this same week was my parents' wedding anniversary. I was able to FaceTime with them while they were out to dinner. Through the screen of my phone, my mom said, "Your dad has something to tell you." She passed the phone to my dad.

"Nikki, I am coming to the Philippines."

I burst into tears and laughter and even let out a squeal of excitement in the middle of Zion Cafe in Chiang Mai, Thailand. I was both shocked and in awe of God. I had fasted and prayed and could see the fruit of it. This made my parents' visit to the Philippines even sweeter, and yet again revealed to me the power of this God I continued to discover.

Three months later, my parents and I were reunited in the Philippines filled with tears of joy, hugs, and kisses. My parents and I, along with the many other racers and their parents, gathered together to go out on mission with Wipe Every Tear. Not only I was going back into the Red Light District, but I had my parents with me. I was grateful for my previous experience in this scene to help my parents with it, which was way out of their comfort zones. From the get-go, Dad was super uncomfortable—and he had every right to be. He pointed out the men his age walking around with young girls. He hated the sight of this and pictured these girls as if they were his own daughters. He was disgusted. He was also uncomfortable because the women tried to get his attention; male clients are how they make most of their money.

We walked into our first bar. We had permission from the ministry to have at least one person in the group order an alcoholic beverage, so we did not raise suspicion. In some countries it's looked down upon for Christians to drink alcohol, however we were undercover. I lead my parents to a table and ordered drinks. In front of us was a stage lined with girls with numbers attached to them. I began to pray as I looked into the eyes of these girls. I stood up and walked toward one girl who caught my eye. She leaned down, and I asked her if she would like to have a drink and sit with me. In order to have time with a girl, we had to buy her a drink. The more drinks we bought, the more time we had with her.

I lead her to the table where my parents were sitting and invited her to join us. I asked her name, about her family, if she had any kids, and what she liked to do in her free time. At first, she seemed nervous and tense. I would be too if I didn't know what to expect, but I kept eye contact with her and smiled and continued to ask questions about her life. I watched her sigh with relief as she became more comfortable. She even ordered a glass of milk.

After sipping her milk, she looked at my parents and me and asked, "What are you doing here? You're different." This was the open door to tell her our reason for being there. We loved Jesus and had an opportunity to offer her education as a way to expand her life. Many of the girls we talked to were hesitant because this offering seemed too good to be true. A safe place to live. Education. Food. Money to support their families. One girl told me they are offered many gifts and promises by men that are constantly broken. With this understanding, I could see their hesitation for our offer.

As we talked about this opportunity, I called over one of the girls who was on staff with Wipe Every Tear. She herself was a former bar girl, but when this same opportunity was presented to her, she took it and it changed her life. She told her story and showed pictures of herself in her school uniform and even her class schedule.

One girl in particular I will never forget because we are

still in contact. My parents and I met her the first night in the first bar we went to. The first girl we talked with grabbed her friend to sit with us. We bought her a drink, too, so we could have time to talk with her. She ordered the same drink as her friend—milk. They both told us how they hated alcohol and all they wanted was something comforting and filling because they were hungry.

The second girl told me her name was "Juicy;" however, I couldn't hear her with the loud music blaring, and I thought she said "Lucy." She later spoke into my ear to tell me her name was "Juicy," but she liked that I called her Lucy.

We talked with the girls for about an hour. I couldn't believe they were my age. I learned about their families and how they are both mothers to young children they left at home with their relatives. How they were in this place to be able to provide for their families, and they didn't see a way out until we came along. I shared with them an opportunity to see the safe houses for themselves. The entire group would be on a bus heading to these houses on Friday morning. I told them the time and place to meet us in hopes to see them there.

Friday morning rolled around and one by one, girls showed up. We filled the bus with seventeen girls from all our various interactions. My heart leapt when Lucy showed up that morning.

God was in this place. The Holy Spirit was at work in the hearts of these young women. God used us to be a light in the darkness and to offer hope. A few of the girls who came with us on the bus stayed at the safe house, never to return to the bar life. God is good!

Lucy and I are friends on Facebook. For about a year after I met her, she continued working in the bar. I'd message her, asking about her life, and she would tell me how she wanted to leave but felt she couldn't because of the money. It broke my heart. She would talk of God and how she felt He was still with her even in the dark place. I would tell her how beautiful, worthy, and valuable she was and how God wanted more for her; but she was right, He is always with her. Now, by the grace of God and His persistent pursuit of her, she is out of the bar, going to school, and is able to spend time with her child! Praise God!

Each night after we returned from the bars, I went to my parents' room to debrief. I shared with them how important it was to talk out loud about certain feelings and thoughts because this helps to process something as intense and foreign as what we experienced. I asked them how they felt, what they were thinking, and then we prayed together. This experience was overstimulating and a lot to take in. It's helpful and healing to express and share what you see, feel, and sense with people you feel safe and trust. I am grateful for these moments with my parents.

A friend of mine who went on the race a different time told me of her experience in the bars. It was also during their PVT. She was with a fellow racer and his parents. They walked into a bar and felt the need to pray for the men. They prayed the men would be convicted of the sin they were in and walk out of the bar. They picked a man out of the crowd and prayed for him to be convicted and leave. Moments later the man got up and quickly made his way out of the bar. The Holy Spirit was on the move.

They pointed out another man and prayed he would be convicted and leave. At first, he didn't move. They continued praying. He didn't move. They prayed more, and just when they were about to lose hope, the man jumped up and ran out of the bar.

I pray the Red Light Districts all over the world will be shut down in Jesus' name and that the Holy Spirit would sweep the streets and conviction would take place in the hearts of everyone there.

A God You've Never Met: Who is the Holy Spirit?

Chapter 17

Light in the Darkness

You are the light of the world. A city on a hill cannot be hidden. Neither do people light a lamp and put it under a bowl. Instead they put it on its stand, and it gives light to everyone in the house. In the same way, let your light shine before men, that they may see your good deeds and praise your Father in heaven.

Matthew 5:14-16

I was called into Rob's office. Rob is originally from the states, a Southern California surfer who moved to Managua, Nicaragua, where he met his wife. They work with a ministry called Breaking Chains, rescuing girls from the sex trafficking industry. Rob is the one who goes into the bars and brothels to rescue girls.

Rob sat in the chair behind his desk with a cigar in his hand. I walked in and stood at the head of his desk, anxiously awaiting what was to come. He told me he has been trying to rescue a few girls who stand on a specific street. He said he had been in contact with the police, and an officer agreed to go with him to document the exact location and file a report of this specific case.

Rob asked if I wanted to accompany him and the officer, along with three other girls from my team. I nodded, unable to really form words, because I really didn't know what we were getting ourselves into. I had turned to walk out the door when he said, "And, we are going tonight." I stopped, spun around, stood in silence for a second before responding, "Ok. Yes! Let's go." He told me the plan and I was instructed to make sure at least two of us in the group spoke some Spanish, and another would be needed to take photos.

I gathered my team of seven to discuss the turn of events for the night. We all agreed Christina and I would be the Spanish speakers, Rachel had a nice camera and was assigned to take photos, and Amanda would come to pray and intercede throughout the operation.

Later that night, Christina, Amanda, Rachel, and I climbed into the back of Rob's Classic Range Rover, which had an extended cab with bench seats facing each other. We filed in and took our seats on the bench. The grocery store was our first stop. Rob picked up cookies and soda to give the girls as our "in" to talk with them. Next, we stopped by the police station to pick up his friend who was an officer. She was dressed in street clothes, to not give away her cover.

On our way to our mission's location, Christina, Rachel, Amanda, and I prayed. We prayed for the Holy Spirit to come. We prayed God would send His angels to protect us and the girls. We had no idea what to expect. As our heads bobbed around in the back of the truck, we looked at each other with wide eyes. What the heck were we getting ourselves into?

Butterflies filled my stomach. This was something Rob and Breaking Chains did often; we just happened to be able to participate this time.

As we continued to pray, Amanda told us she saw angels surrounding the vehicle. I felt a sense of peace, and the voice of God telling us we had nothing to be afraid of because He was with us. We were to bring His light into the darkness.

We pulled up where we saw two young girls, no older than fourteen. Christina and I were instructed to offer the girls cookies and talk with them in their native language and get any information we could on the situation. All the while, we could not be seen by the "customers" and had to make sure the young girls were facing the car so Rachel could snap photos of their faces for the investigation.

Christina and I jumped out of the vehicle with cookies and soda in hand. My heart pounded, not only because it was late at night, but also because of the trafficking activity we knew was going on throughout the neighborhood. I could feel the evil all around me.

These little girls wore short skirts, shirts that showed their midriffs, and high heels, and stood with their arms across their bodies. They looked scared, and as soon as we pulled up, terror shown through their eyes. For all they knew, they were getting picked up by a customer. Christina and I walked around from the back of the car with cookies, soda, and smiling faces. Their demeanor instantly changed.

Christina and I had been told three girls usually stand together in this specific spot. I asked the girls who they were waiting for, and they told us they were waiting for their customers; one of their sisters was already working. My heart sank. I tried to stay composed, but my heart broke inside. It felt so surreal. Was this really happening? The whole situation was like a scene from a movie. We couldn't stay long, because we knew the traffickers were close by and these girls had to work to make money. If they didn't, they would be beaten—or worse.

Everything in me wanted to take these two young girls with us to safety, but that was not our mission that night. Our mission was to gather evidence. Rob assured us he would be back to rescue all three of the girls. It's all about timing.

I am not fluent in Spanish by any means. I can get by. I understand more than I can actually speak; however, in that moment I felt the Holy Spirit come upon me and gave me more of a Spanish vocabulary. I was able to talk with these precious girls and understand everything they were telling us. The Holy Spirit was with us for sure! "...the Holy Spirit will teach you at the time what you should say" (Luke 12:12b). After about five minutes, Christina and I got back into the car. My heart was pounding. Rachel had gotten the photos and the police could now file a report.

As I think back on this experience, my heart breaks, picturing the innocent faces of those girls. Trafficking happens all around us, even in the United States. There is darkness in this world, and we need to be aware of it. However, like Jesus tells us in the Bible, we carry light within us. That night, we were in the darkness, but as we approached these girls, they saw something different in us.

In the book titled *The Veil*, Blake Healy shares about his ability to see in the spiritual realm. He sees angels and demons. He writes how the spiritual realm is more real than the physical, and we all have the ability to see it if we lift our veils. He described a time when a group of believers were walking down a street in Venice Beach, California. As they walked, a stream of light followed them. Everywhere they walked the light followed and touched the people in their path. There was freshness in the atmosphere as they walked down the dark street.

This is something I have been praying for. I want a light to follow me. I want the atmosphere to shift when I walk in. When people see me, I want them to see Jesus and feel the presence of the Holy Spirit. In the Bible, as Paul walked down the street, his shadow healed people because he had the power and authority of the Holy Spirit. Let's be lights in this dark world and share light everywhere we go. There is a power within you. Do you realize the kind of power you carry?

A God You've Never Met: Who is the Holy Spirit?

Chapter 18

The Power Within

...And his incomparably great power for us who believe. That power is like the working of his mighty strength...

Ephesians 1:19

In the book of John, Jesus says, "The wind blows wherever it pleases. You hear its sound, but you cannot tell where it comes from or where it is going. So it is with everyone born of the Spirit" (John 3:8). We see the effects of the Holy Spirit, but we don't actually see *Him*. Our faith is of the unseen. Most of us don't see in the supernatural, we see in the natural, as with someone's leg healed, someone's back relieved of pain, or in shaking, falling over, or laughing.

There are examples of this in Scripture. In Matthew 18:1-6, Judas betrays Jesus, and the man who seizes Jesus falls back when Jesus says, "I am he." In Matthew 28:1-4, the guards near the tomb shake and become as "dead men." This still happens today by the power of the Holy Spirit.

This power is within you. I think most followers of Jesus don't realize the power they carry. The access you have is to *the* all-powerful and mighty One. I didn't realize this either. When I would see others perform miracles and healings, prophesy and speak in tongues, at the time, I didn't realize I had the same access. And even still I have to remind myself of this power. To be honest, I don't fully walk in it as I should.

We underestimate His power and the power within us. I've heard people tell stories of miracles taking place in a "healing room." People begin to think they have to go to this "room" to experience the power of God—and that's not true! The people in these places continually cultivate a space for the Holy Spirit to move.

We have the same access to the same God with the same power. You don't have to go anywhere to experience this, you just have to create a space for Him to move. Open up your heart and mind to Him and the impossible will happen.

In Luke 1, Mary talks about how the Lord uses a humble servant like herself to carry the King into this world. And she addresses God as the *Mighty One*. I looked through other scriptures addressing God as *mighty*. There are multiple places where the psalmists mention God as the one who *speaks and summons the earth* (Psalm 50:1); *mighty and his faithfulness surrounds him* (Psalm 89:8); *he is mighty in power* (Psalm 147:5); *his understanding has no limit* (Psalm 147:5). And we have access to this power. God asked me this question and it may be one for you to ask yourself, "You have access to me and my power, why don't you utilize it?"

I believe this starts with realizing how valuable and important you are as a person. When we acknowledge our value and worth, we believe in our right as Christians to use the power living inside of us. The Holy Spirit is of the supernatural, and we need to start living our lives in the physical and supernatural. We need to be the same person in every aspect of our lives and invite the Holy Spirit into each one.

We need to get out of our own way. Fear holds us back from experiencing this power. Ask yourself these questions. *What is holding me back from praying for the impossible? Why am I afraid to be unstoppable with the Holy Spirit's power?*

I often think about how unstoppable I can be with the Holy Spirit. With God all things are possible. When we put expectations on God, we put Him in a box. We limit Him. Do not underestimate the power that lives within you. His name is the Holy Spirit. Through Him, miracles happen. Through Him, people's dreams become reality. Are you living a life using the power within?

The Holy Spirit resides in those who accept Jesus as their Savior, and their body then becomes a temple of the Holy Spirit.

Do you not know that your body is a temple of
the Holy Spirit, who is in you,
Whom you have received from God?

1 Corinthians 6:19

The body we have on this earth, was given to us as a gift, and it is a storehouse of the Holy Spirit. Ephesians 2:20 says Jesus Himself is the foundation, and in Him the whole building is joined together, which is the holy temple. In verse 22, we are mentioned as being built together with Christ to become a dwelling place for the Spirit of God to live. The Spirit of the living God is living inside every believer!

Think about your body for a moment. Do you love your body? Are you confident in your body? Do you take care of it in a way that pleases the Lord, as though it is a storehouse of His Spirit?

I have struggled with this time and again. This knowledge plays a huge role in how we carry ourselves in the name of Jesus, and how we use the power of the Holy Spirit.

I have been on a health journey from the inside out. I struggled with loving myself in how I looked in the past, because I knew that's not where I wanted to stay. And yet I struggled with taking action to change. It takes time and effort, but it starts with loving yourself in the place you are in now.

Look at yourself in the mirror. Do you love the person staring back at you? I know at times I do, and other times I don't. Look at yourself in the mirror again and see yourself as someone who is carrying the Holy Spirit. Do you look at yourself differently? I know I do. This is something I need to remind myself each day. How I care for myself is a reflection of how important it is to me that I carry the Holy Spirit inside of me. I want my body to be a place of health, healing, and freedom.

Your body is a temple of the Holy Spirit and you should treat it as such. To be your best and serve others in the best way, you must honor the fleshly body God has given you. First Corinthians 6:20 tells us to "honor God" with our bodies. How are you honoring God today? Take steps to become better and better each day, but love yourself in the process. Do it for the Holy Spirit who is living inside of you and the power you carry!

Chapter 19

Hearing God's Voice

After the earthquake came a fire, but the Lord was not in the fire. And after the fire came a gentle whisper.

1 Kings 19:12

Many people ask me, how do you hear God's voice? What does His voice sound like?

I have never heard the audible voice of God. For me, it's more like a feeling and a whisper.[51] But you may be wondering, how do you decipher between your own voice and God's?

There are times in my earlier life God was speaking to me, but I didn't know it. At the time it was more of a conviction, knowing what was right and wrong. It was a feeling of peace in a room of chaos. It was the smile of a small child when I served abroad. It is selfless love. I started to see the commonality in these situations and searched for the same voice in my head or feeling in my heart during these times.

51 *Whisper: Hearing the Voice of God* by Mark Batterson

There have been many times I was confused about which voice was mine and which was God's. Moments of debate whether the Spirit of God was telling me to do something or if it was me. Later in my life, I realized I needed to dive deeper into a practical way to hear the voice of God. I decided I needed to create space and be disciplined. I want to share with you what I did, because it may be helpful for you.

I sat in my room, surrounded by complete silence. I had a journal and pen in hand and began writing all the words that came to me. I wrote whatever thoughts were in my head. I needed to clear space for God to speak, and at the moment my own thoughts were getting in the way.

I continued to sit in silence and moved my thoughts to think only about God. This whole process took time and the effort of carving out silent space in my day. We live in a world of distractions and noise. We must silence ourselves to be able to hear the whisper of God. He could speak in a booming voice, but He chooses not to. He wants us to quiet ourselves, seek Him, and then He will speak. He is speaking to us all the time, but we have such noise in our lives, we must be intentional to listen. He wants for us to sit at His feet and be present with Him.

When I was thinking only about God, I paid attention to the words that came next and wrote them down. This time something was different; the words only came to me as I wrote them down. Another word or phrase wouldn't come until I had written the words in my head first. I was shocked when I went back to read what I had written. What I had written I would have never come up with on my own. I wrote words for other people, words about other's lives, and words about my own life.

I have practiced this over and over again and continue

to do it to this day. I understand there are times it's hard to find a silent place. A year later, while I was on the World Race, I was constantly around other people. I could never go anywhere by myself. The only way I could get away from the others was to sit with headphones on and listen to music. And that's ok! I think God just wants to spend time with us, and if we concentrate and listen for His whisper, He will honor that and speak.

There have been times I would question if what I was hearing was God or some other voice, and in those times, I notice a common theme. If it's my voice, I allow my selfish desires to get in the way and think of what I want and not what God wants for me. And let me tell you, it doesn't end well. But there's grace, and God is a gracious Father. Sometimes we need to stop directing our conversations by asking God for this or that, and instead sit, listen, and be still. He knows the desires of your heart (Psalm 37:3). Allow Him to speak to you. It's a precious time.

In Mark Batterson's book *Whisper: Hearing the Voice of God*, he writes, "If you want to hear the heart of God, silence is key. If you want the Spirit of God to fill you, be still."

A few years ago, I went on a mission trip to Belize. During this trip, it was important to me to find space to be alone with Jesus. Searching for a place away from the others, I wandered into the building where we had our group meetings and worship time. There was a ladder that led to a loft. I had my Bible and journal in hand and climbed this ladder to find a table with a chair. This was perfect! I sat in the chair, put my headphones in, and turned on worship music.

First, I sat with my eyes closed and began to pray. I asked Jesus and the Holy Spirit to meet me there. I started with journaling about my experiences on the trip so far, and asked

God to speak to me.

As I wrote and prayed, I had a sense I was not alone. But I wasn't afraid. No one else was there when my eyes were open. But I closed my eyes and saw Jesus standing beside me. He placed His hand on my shoulder. Joy overcame me. I was speechless, and yet all I could do was laugh. Tears filled my eyes and rolled down my cheeks as I sat in the moment. I was in awe of what was happening.

When Jesus placed His hand on my shoulder, it felt like a human hand was touching me. This physical touch is something I had been praying for many years prior to this encounter. I had heard people tell stories of their own encounters like this with Jesus and I wanted it to happen for myself. In this moment it did! I didn't want it to end. I was in the presence of Jesus.

Jesus wants to be with you and He wants you to feel His presence. This may look different for each individual. You may experience Him through a verse in the Bible, through a friend, through His creation, through those quiet moments in your living room, or in another country sitting in a loft. He is everywhere, but it's up to you to create the space for Him to show you.

I once talked with a friend about how she hears God's voice. She said, "It's when I'm doing something like washing the dishes, and then BAM! He says something that hits me dead in my tracks. I am not one to write, but I hear His voice when I'm doing other things."

He may speak to you as He does my friend. He is always talking to us, but it's our job to tune our ear to His voice. The Bible says Jesus is the shepherd and His sheep know His voice.[52] Do you know your shepherd's voice? Are you

52 John 10:4

spending the time you need to discern His voice from others? God tells us to "Be still and know that I am God."[53] Jesus talks about being the "Good Shepherd" and the "gate for the sheep." In John 10, Jesus says His sheep listen to His voice and follow Him because they know His voice.[54] If we are to be followers of Jesus, we need to know what His voice sounds like.

Someone once told me, when a sheep continues to do something the shepherd does not want because it is not safe for the sheep, the shepherd breaks its leg so it cannot walk. The shepherd then carries the sheep on his shoulders everywhere he goes until the sheep is healed. When the sheep is healed and can walk on its own again, it stays close to the shepherd and follows him because it knows the shepherd's voice. This sheep has been on the shoulders of the shepherd and has heard his voice constantly for a significant amount of time and now obeys what its shepherd says to do. During this time, the sheep has learned the shepherd protects and wants what's best for the sheep.

This is how we must be with Jesus. He is our shepherd and we need to stay close to Him. We need to understand he is not out to hurt us, but wants what's best for us. This will take time and effort, but those are necessary to truly know the voice of God.

A practical way to do this is by creating a space of stillness and minimal distractions. Here's how I do that. I put my phone on airplane mode thirty minutes before I go to sleep, and I don't turn it back on until after my quiet time in the morning. If you don't want to put your phone on airplane mode, put it on silent and flip your phone over so you won't be distracted

53 Psalm 46:10

54 John 10:14

by notifications. God wants our undivided attention, and the only way to learn what His voice sounds like is to give Him attention and time. I know for me, when I am talking with a friend and that person is looking at her phone, I feel she doesn't care about what I have to say, or she doesn't want to engage with me. Think of this in regard to being present with God. To hear His voice, you must practice, be disciplined, be present and limit your distractions.

Chapter 20

In the Little Things

But the Advocate, the Holy Spirit, whom the Father will send in my name, will teach you all things and will remind you of everything I have said to you.

John 14:26

As I was talking to a friend about this book and the topic of the Holy Spirit, this friend told me how wonderful it was I was writing about the Holy Spirit because many people might experience Him without knowing it. Let's talk about the ways you might experience Him.

Have you ever been singing or soaking in worship and get goose bumps? This is a move of the Holy Spirit.

Have you ever stood in worship and can't stop smiling? Holy Spirit. Or crying, for that matter? Holy Spirit.

Have you ever been washing dishes and a friend pops into your head? Holy Spirit prompting you to pray for that person.

Have you seen a homeless man on the side of the road

and drive right past him, but you have a tug to go back? Holy Spirit.

Have you ever been sitting in the midst of creation and had a sense of peace and awe? Holy Spirit.

Have you ever been walking along the beach and looked out at the ocean to see dolphins leaping above the water? If you are like me, this brings you great joy; and yes, that is the Holy Spirit.

The moment when your heart starts pounding out of your chest and you feel you may burst unless you speak up! Holy Spirit.

When a word is spoken to you so specific to your life it leaves you speechless. The Holy Spirit speaking through someone is known as prophecy.

The Holy Spirit speaks to us and gets our attention in many different ways. This is the beauty of Him. He is everywhere, and most times He speaks to us in ways that would only get our personal attention. Sometimes when He communicates with us, it's not with words. For example, seeing dolphins while surfing or walking along the beach. The Holy Spirit knows how significant this is to me and this shows me He is with me.

I was out in the water on my surfboard when some dolphins swam past me. I paddled deeper toward them so I could get a closer look. All the other surfers were paddling to get waves, but not me; I was paddling to see dolphins. This was the Holy Spirit interacting with me in a way only I would understand.

Open up your eyes to see how He is communicating with you and trying to get your attention. I pray you see Him in a personal way, something special between you and Him.

The Holy Spirit is in the little things, which I found to be true while I was in Cambodia. As I sat in that storage room, I had a divine encounter with the Holy Spirit. When I heard the words in the song I was listening to, "You are my anchor in the wind and the waves," I thought of what an anchor represents. I thought of God being my anchor, keeping me grounded in storms.

I love the ocean, which I also think of when I hear the word or see a picture of an anchor. For a split second I had the thought, *an anchor would be a cool tattoo.* I grew up in a home where tattoos were frowned upon and I never wanted to disappoint my parents, so I didn't let myself think about even getting one. This was the first time I had thought about it.

A month prior, I'd had a dream about getting a tattoo. It was a small tattoo on the inside of my left ankle, but I couldn't make out what it was. In my dream, I was filled with regret immediately and worried about what others would think of me.

I didn't revisit this thought until five months later. I was in my eleventh and final month of the World Race. We were in Durban, South Africa, for a few days of debrief before heading back to the States. I was sitting with Erica in our room and she mentioned getting a tattoo to represent this life changing experience. I mentioned to her my tattoo idea from months before and she lit up with excitement. She knew my upbringing and stance regarding tattoos. She had heard me more than once say I would never get one.

I told Erica I was thinking of an anchor on my ankle somewhere. To help make my decision, she drew a small anchor in the place I'd likely have it. For the next three days, I intensely prayed over this idea. I would look down at the drawing and ask God what I should do. For those three days, this seemed to be all I could think of and pray about. During those days, God told me over and over, *It's not that big of a deal. Don't worry about what others think. This is between you and me.* And He was right. Deep down, I was dealing with my desire to please others including my parents. I didn't want to disappoint them. But God is my top priority and the one I need to listen to at all costs. And if He says it's not that big of a deal, then why not?

At the end of those three days of dialogue with God, I told Erica, "Let's do it!" We headed into town to look for a tattoo artist. We came across a Victorian-style house that had been converted into a tattoo parlor. We walked inside and saw a young man about our age at the front desk. Tattoos covered his body. He introduced himself and we discussed our designs with him.

As we talked, he commented how there were many foreigners and asked if we were all together. Erica and I giggled and said yes. He asked why we were there, and I told him, "We are Christian missionaries and have been away from home for eleven months, but we are heading back to the States this week!"

He was a bit shocked and said, "But you seem so normal and cool. You're really missionaries?" Erica and I looked at each other and back at our new friend as we smiled and nodded. He told us about a time he went to church, which was only because his girlfriend at the time wanted him to go. He said it wasn't for him. We weren't there to push Jesus on him, and we weren't there to tell him what was right, so we told him that was ok. When we did, it was as though something changed in him, and he let out a sigh and smiled. He told us to come back the following day, and as we left, we were excited for what was to come.

The next day, Erica and I walked back to the Victorian house tattoo parlor and followed Shelby into his art room.

As he opened the door, drawings of Satan and demons hung upon the walls. I giggled out of shock to myself and silently prayed. *Holy Spirit come.* Shelby told us he had drawn those himself. In that moment, I knew Erica and I were there for more than getting tattoos.

As he set up, he told us he usually plays hardcore metal music, but he thought he shouldn't this time. I politely smiled and looked at Erica with a sigh of relief. Erica went first. She got three birds on her shoulder to represent the Father, Son, and Holy Spirit. As he drew each bird, she silently prayed for him to have a relationship with each member of the Trinity.

During this time together, she and I asked about his life, getting to know him and making jokes together. It was quite enjoyable. Soon, it was my turn. I was excited and nervous at the same time. I was about to do something I always told myself I would never do, but also felt peace and a calm about following through. The Holy Spirit was present in that moment and I knew this was bigger than myself and even bigger than the tiny anchor on the inside of my left ankle.

When he was finished, we smiled and laughed and even took a photo together. He walked us out to the front door and with a smile on his face said, "Thank you for blessing me with your presence." I smiled with joy. We not only got tattoos, but we were a light and brought the Holy Spirit with us. When God told me it wasn't a big deal and it was between me and Him, in those moments with this man I knew this to be true.

Years later, I still love my little anchor. It reminds me of this story and the other stories I had a privilege of being a part of while on the race. It also reminds me of the power of God, Jesus, and the Holy Spirit, in whom I am anchored. This little anchor has been a great conversation starter to tell people about Jesus!

Nikki Romani   147

One thing I learned through all of this is to listen to God and not others. He will tell you what you need to do. And trust me, when you do, it will be life-changing. The Holy Spirit is in the little things. Be aware of His movement around you, even in a tattoo parlor.

Chapter 21

With Obedience Comes Reward

The Lord will establish you as his holy people, as he promised you on oath, if you keep the commands of the Lord your God and walk in obedience to him. Then all the peoples on earth will see that you are called by the name of the Lord, and they will fear you.

Deuteronomy 28:9-10

With faith comes obedience and with obedience comes reward and walking in the Spirit.

There is importance in seeking God in all we do, inviting Him into our decisions and seeking His wisdom and discernment in every situation. There comes a time when you hear Him say something to you and you think, *there's no way He wants me to do that, right?* And in that moment, it is our decision to obey Him or not to obey Him.

It's a scary thing sometimes. I think back to when I was researching about the World Race. I could have continued to research, avoided the push, and not take action, but deep down I knew I would be disobeying God. It was scary, and I had no idea what I was getting myself into, but with risk comes reward, and that's exactly what happened. It was not the easiest time of my life, but I am so glad I was obedient to God's push to go. All the signs pointed to yes and I got to the point I couldn't ignore them anymore. It was as though if I ignored His signs, I would feel horrible.

I also think about God calling me to write this book. When He first told me to write a book, I ignored Him. I pushed this idea to the side for two whole months. And each time in those two months when I sat with Jesus and asked Him how to share with more people about the Holy Spirit, He would tell me to write a book.

You know what finally made me decide to accept this responsibility? God told me He was going to give this opportunity to someone else. Heck no! In that moment I sat up straighter, and in confidence I told God, "No! I will do it!" And I am so glad I did. This has been a challenging, humbling, and growing experience. I have learned more about myself and God in the process. Writing has created a space for me to process, to heal, and required discipline to actually sit down and write, even when I didn't have the words to say. But I had you in mind the whole time.

Is God calling you into something that scares you? Do you feel His nudge or conviction to say yes, but you are letting fear get in the way? Honestly, I am still learning to say yes with abandon, but the more I say yes, the stronger I become; the deeper my faith grows; and the more I learn about God, Jesus, and the Holy Spirit.

You may be wondering, *How do I know when I am listening to God and obeying Him or not?* You will know! We discussed hearing the voice of God and feeling convicted by the Holy Spirit. Sometimes you have to pull the trigger and do it messy to figure out what He is calling you to do. You may have no clue, but you won't figure it out until you try something. It's a safe bet if it scares you, you should do it. Getting out of your comfort zone is a great way to obey the call of God on your life. The Holy Spirit is our guide, counselor, and confidant. Go to Him and He will navigate life with you.

With obedience comes spiritual maturity. Mark Batterson writes, "Your enjoyment level of spending time with God determines your spiritual maturity."[55] Obeying God should be your greatest joy.

Notice I didn't say *easiest?* It's not going to be easy, but it should bring us great joy because we are serving a God who loves us. And because it brings us joy, it won't matter how hard or uncomfortable it is.

I needed to get myself out of the way and see the true reason God wanted me to write in the first place. It's all because of you. Thinking of you is what kept me going. Thinking of your life and how important it is and how much God loves you is why I continued to write. I have prayed many times to see people the way God sees them, and to have His heart. And He loves you so much and wants to reveal Himself to you in a fresh and new way.

My prayer is this book opens the door to a refreshed relationship with your Lord and Savior. That it ignites a fire within you. My hope is you realize you are important, you are special, and God has an amazing plan for your life. The Holy Spirit wants you to know He is living inside of you, and He is

55 *Whisper: Hearing the Voice of God* by Mark Batterson

waiting for you to unleash the power within. You can change the world, but it starts with your relationship with the One who created you. You are precious to Him. He loves you. And He wants to go on this journey with you. No more sitting on the fence. It's time to experience a God you've never met.

Acknowledgements

I would have never been able to do this on my own. God gave me the confidence and the strength to keep going, the Holy Spirit guided me along on this unknown journey, and Jesus sat with me so I never felt alone.

To my Grandma, for leaving behind documents about her life and articles she collected about the Holy Spirit. She and I wrote this together. To my Mama, you are my biggest cheerleader, and the one I can call upon at any moment to pray for me. I know you always have my back. To my Dad, you are supportive and loving even if you don't understand what I'm doing. You sacrifice so much to provide for our family. Parents, I am forever grateful. I am who I am today because of you!

To my prayer and support team, I would not have been able to get through those hard moments and spiritual warfare without you. To my cousin Kristin for proofreading and constant belief in me to be able to do this. To my editor, Anna Floit, you helped me articulate what I wanted to say and put it into book form. Shout out to my A Squad family from the World Race. Many of these stories are because we said "yes" to God calling us to take a risk, and I am forever grateful for each of you.

To my family, for always supporting me no matter what crazy adventure I go on. To Rachel, my life with the Holy Spirit is because you pushed me to experience more and I am forever grateful. I love you sister-best friend! To my girls from PLNU and my soul sisters (you know who you are), thanks for encouraging me and praying for me. Life is better with you in it.

This has been an exciting, challenging adventure. I had no idea what I was getting myself into, but let me tell you, you never know what will happen when the Holy Spirit is leading. I took a risk and do not regret it and I am forever grateful for the community surrounding me.

About the Author

Nikki Romani is a certified life coach and athletic trainer. She helps individuals find their identity in Jesus, and shares the importance of caring for themselves mind, body, and spirit. She helps athletes comeback after injury with a new understanding of who they are. Nikki is host of the True Identity Podcast and lives in San Diego, California where she enjoys playing outside in the sunshine and visiting the ocean close by.

Made in the USA
San Bernardino, CA
21 March 2020